Walk the Goddess Walk . . .

Pia Jacobs

call me

text me

email me

tweet me

Google me

pia...me

*A fashion
and lifestyle guide
for girls who aspire
to be their best*

Pia Jacobsen

Illustrations by Zang Toi

Order this book online at www.trafford.com
or email orders@trafford.com

Most Trafford titles are also available at major online book retailers.

Printed in Victoria, BC, Canada.

ISBN: 978-1-4269-2727-0 (dj)

*Our mission is to efficiently provide the world's finest, most comprehensive
book publishing service, enabling every author to experience success.
To find out how to publish your book, your way, and have it available
worldwide, visit us online at www.trafford.com*

Trafford rev. 03/15/2010

 www.trafford.com

North America & international
toll-free: 1 888 232 4444 (USA & Canada)
phone: 250 383 6864 • fax: 812 355 4082

pia...me

*A fashion
and lifestyle guide
for girls who aspire
to be their best*

Pia Jacobsen

Table of Contents

Foreword

As an eveningwear designer with over thirty years in the fashion business, I have had the great pleasure of dressing some of the world's most glamorous women. It's not the models and celebrities that I think about when designing, it's the thousands of women I meet every year who come to me for the "red carpet moments" of their lives that I have in mind.

From my days at the houses of Nina Ricci and Dior to my two decades designing under my own name, I have never come across anyone of Pia's quiet, confident, and discerning taste level. Pia and I spent many hours in my showroom editing my collections while she was a buyer for one of my first major retailers. Her high standards and unerring eye coupled with a passion for great design make her an ideal sage of fashion wisdom. This book will dramatically affect young women's choices by encouraging them to define who they aspire to be and how they project themselves to the world.

I really can't think of a better person to offer styling advice to young women.

Carmen Marc Valvo

The Porcelain Doll

I was four years old when I was caught red-handed playing with my older sister's porcelain bride doll. The doll was exquisite, perfection really. Her skin was flawless, her hair blond with silken curls that flattered her dark eyes framed in long lashes. The lips were so pouty and pink. The white lace and beaded gown with yes, a matching veil that was as long as her hair.

How could I resist? I looked at her admiringly, and touched her ever so tentatively. We had whispered secrets to share and the promise of being best friends forever.

Actually, I was found with her several times in my sister's bedroom. The forbidden fruit. After much begging, whining, pleading, pining, whimpering, and generally being a total pain, my parents bought me my very own bride doll for Christmas. That was when I first learned at the age of four, that whining can get you what you want.

It was love at first sight. She was a brunette, and much thinner than my sister's doll. Her features were sharper and she was way more sophisticated. Her white dress and veil were scratchy yet fabulous at the same time. She had a bit of an edge that seemed to make her superior to the sweet, soft, refined and elegant other one. She smelled differently, too. I was in heaven that Christmas morning, and I couldn't wait to show her off to my cool older cousin, Marney. I sat with her on Christmas Day in the back of our new Chevy station wagon, on the way to my Auntie Marge and Uncle Bill's for dinner.

When my father turned a sharp corner, the station wagon swerved, and my bride's arm flung up and hit me smack dab in the face with such a force it made me go cross-eyed. Instinctively, in a split second and as a reaction to being hit, I quickly grabbed her hand and bit off her fingers.

Yes, off.

All her fingers, each and every one – intense moment by intense moment – on that sorry hand. That wasn't even the worst part. It felt so good to do it – that was the best part. They were hollow and chewy. Better in my mouth, than on the hand of this stupid, plastic doll.

While I did not realize it then, this was my *aha* moment, when things of quality took their firm hold on me. A therapist might say I bit the fingers of the doll off in a moment of anger – furious the doll had hit me – or that I was jealous of my sister. But I now know better: quality is something I recognized even then, and was something of importance to me. I wanted the porcelain bride doll, because she was elegant, refined, had softer features, a better figure, smelled better, and had silkier hair. Her dress was made of a softer fabric, even the lace on her veil was B-E-T-T-E-R – I just knew it! My bride was not porcelain at all. She was, alas, mere plastic. No matter how beautiful and brand-new my bride doll was, she would never be the elegant and precious one. Hence, my pursuit of quality and all things beautiful.

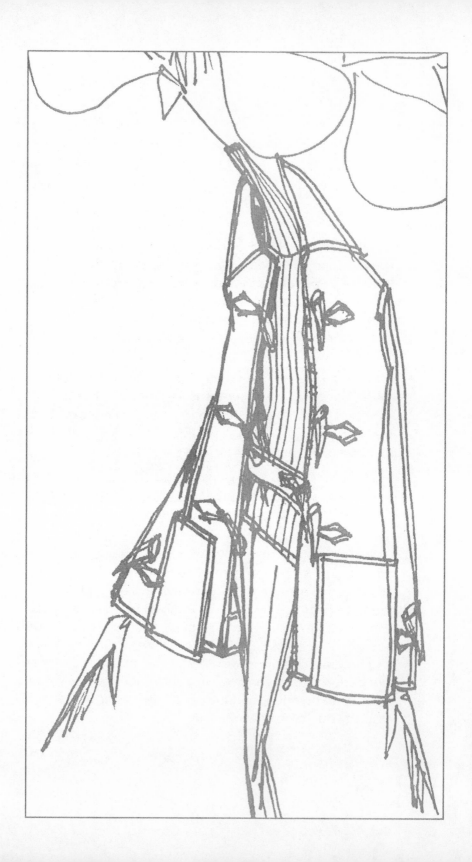

You and Your Look

Who are you? What is important to you? How do you choose to portray yourself to the world?

Big questions to be sure, but important ones. By getting to know ourselves intimately and figuring out what our likes and dislikes are early on in life, it all becomes purposeful. Knowing what you want, and who you are is key. While not a simple feat, doing so will provide the boundaries and establish the parameters by which to make decisions and ultimately live by. If you hold yourself to your dreams, it makes life so much more clear. Ask yourself, will this help to get me to where I want to go? Am I taking the easy way out now, only to make it more difficult for me to get back on track later? The ways we look and act play an integral part in supporting our decisions.

If you are dressing like a punk rocker, it works if you want a music career as a punk rocker. It doesn't work if you want to be a financial analyst. Which reminds me of a party I attended in Paris after Stella McCartney's design debut at the spectacular Opéra Garnier (I'm going to shamelessly drop names). Directly across the aisle from me in living color was her dad, Paul McCartney, plus Ringo Starr and his wife Barbara Bach, a.k.a. Bond Girl #whatever. Two Beatles and a babe. I have to admit, it was a bit distracting. Anyway, when I walked into the after-party, there was Sir Paul, "standing right in front of me." (Everything you say just happens to be from the lyrics to a Beatles song.) All I could do was smile and say "hello." But what I really noticed were his feet. He was wearing high-top tennis shoes with a suit. This is adorable and works if you are 17. Not quite the same effect at, what, 60? Not that he still wasn't cute, mind you, but you get the point. Your look will need to be updated and brought current on a regular basis.

Everyone approaches life from a different point of view. Vive la différence. We don't all think alike, look alike, or ... follow the same trends, thank god. Variety is the spice of life, but please, let's be smart about our decisions. Dressing like you lost a bet, or that you are always on your way to the gym sends the message that you don't care about the way you look. Learn to embrace your individuality, and if you hear yourself saying yes to wearing yoga pants to places other than to yoga, tell yourself to shut up.

Look, you want to maximize your assets in every way to help you get what you want in life. All you can hope for is to be the absolute best you possibly can be. Why would you want to present yourself in any other light?

Whether you are too big, too small or just right, the key is to be realistic and objective about what you look like. Know your strengths and weaknesses. Dress to accentuate the positive, minimize the negative. All too often, we do not see our accurate reflection when we look in the mirror. Maybe it is just my former anorexic bout returning to haunt me, but when I look in the mirror I sometimes see a really fat, frumpy old lady. It is a recurring nightmare.

ALWAYS look in the rear view mirror before leaving the house. Be sure to have a full-length mirror somewhere in your home. It is a beauty essential. The best type of mirror is a three-way mirror that enables you to see the back side of yourself. I know, the world would be better without this, but we need to know what others are seeing, even if we cringe when we do. To fully utilize a three-way mirror, look straight ahead into one of the side panels, and adjust it while looking forward. Then, check out your derrière, and ask yourself what impression am I leaving? Are you wearing the right lingerie? No lumps, sags, or bulges? Cut tags out of clothes or be sure they are tucked in. I always love an exit dress leaving the restaurant. Back detail can be so interesting and unexpectedly sexy, but you must know what your back actually looks like. So if you have a lot of moles, breakouts, scars or tattoos, we'd rather not see it. Remember to moisturize your back. When you return home, look in the mirror again, and if things don't look as good as they did when you left, it didn't work. At the very least this can be a learning experience.

Have a trusted friend take a full-length photograph of you in a bathing suit or your underwear. This works. You are now a blank canvas, a stunning, striking blank canvas.

Are your shoulders wider than your hips? If so, good for you! Are your legs long, short, or somewhere in between? How do you feel about your breasts? Are they too small in proportion to your hips? Does your tummy protrude further than your breasts? Is your derrière flat, round or somewhere in between? If not, there are things you can do. By choosing the right clothing and the correct proportions, you create a trompe l'oeil effect (pretentious French meaning to make things look different than they really are). You can balance the effect by wearing the right things.

You need to be cognizant of your strengths and areas that are perhaps less strong and how it all works together. Yes, diet and exercise will enhance our best physical features, besides making you live longer, be happier and make your girlfriends jealous of you, but you already know all that. So, knowing what to wear and knowing how to wear it can take you even further towards projecting the image you want.

If you can find your look, that which makes you feel fabulous for nearly every occasion, you are miles ahead of the pack. Establishing your look helps you save money, too, as you are not making as many wardrobe mistakes, and you'll have more money for shoes. For example, if you are more classic, a great pair of charcoal grey pants and charcoal grey cashmere sweater, black pumps, important handbag, and one quality piece of jewelry or a fabulous silk scarf, and you can go anywhere. Foolproof.

Now let's talk fashion magazines, truly an addiction for me. In truth, I tend to look to the ads more than the actual editorial. Until your eye becomes extremely well-trained, it is difficult to decipher the photos. These are very high-fashion, designer pieces that often take one to several seasons to trickle down to mainstream fashion, or they become so watered down you wouldn't recognize them as the same thing. You know how this works, right? Those wacky, far out expensive, haute-couture pieces made of peacock feathers on long-legged, giraffe types standing in abandoned cement factories – no one expects everyone is going to buy one of these. It is a very miniscule percentage of women in the world that can actually afford the couture pieces shown on the editorial pages of high fashion magazines like Vogue. You would need to be able to: 1. Afford these pieces; and 2. Have somewhere to wear them. Even the celebrities are given them to wear on loan from the designers in exchange for the publicity. But these designers are also setting trends that will be copied and modified in their own diffusion lines, like Donna Karan has DKNY and Dolce and Gabbana has D&G, or even by other labels who will copy and sell them for less. Then those designs in some form end up in stores everywhere from Macy's and Nordstrom to H&M and BCBG, and before you know it, you are wearing a watered-down, commercial version of it, but you've got the look for a lot less money.

To interpret the editorial looks into everyday attire, first pay attention to what the specific statement or message is from the editor. What is new about it? Is it a new proportion and the way the pieces fit on the body? Where does the top hit in relation to the bottom? What is the heel height worn with it? Or, it may be about a specific designer's influence for the "season," albeit fall, winter, spring, or summer. It may be a color trend, a pattern, or a social or cultural influence, but often the new fashion message is about proportion. When I look through a magazine, I know not everything will work for me, with respect to my figure and my personal style. Some seasons, there just isn't much that will work for me, and others there are tons. One season for example, the gladiator shoe was everywhere. Well, my legs happen to be slightly short in comparison to my long torso. So the high ankle straps of the gladiators shorten my leg. Now, there may be an alternative that conveys the idea of the sandal without the ankle strap, but I don't really need them, and would rather wait until I see something I can't live without. Even though it is "the look," it may not be my look. I am classic, and I want the world to see me as I see myself: sensible, smart, chic and confident, whether or not I really am. If I am going out and want to have more fun, I might wear some color, like a bright shoe that makes me feel like having fun. I might want to look trendier on occasion, so will add a piece that way. I might put on something sexier if I am going out with my husband on a date night. Always the same classic theme, but by adding a piece or two or changing it up a bit, I stretch to my mood or the occasion.

Make A Statement

For some reason, when the stars are aligned all is good with the world. At the same time, you can go to your closet and pull out an outfit and it just all works, you feel great, get the job or the guy and life is good. This doesn't just happen by accident you know. Once you get it all together, you know what you want, who you are and where you are going, and your look becomes solidified. That is, if you have a look.

I was meeting one of my BFFs in San Francisco at Postrio for a cocktail. Undoubtedly, I looked really chic: black cashmere turtleneck, black pants, black high-heeled boots, black shawl. My chemically treated blond hair was pulled back into a low ponytail, and my lips were perfectly outlined and blazing red. I walked into the restaurant, and was shocked when I saw my friend was wearing exactly what I was. She looked better than I did, too! What can you do? People tend to be sheep, following trends, and what we see on someone else. For the most part we think if something looks good on that girl, it will on me, but that isn't always the case.

It is vital to step out and make a statement of your own. Don't limit yourself. As your confidence grows, so will the compliments. Then what begins to happen is the whole point of all of this. If you are organized, thoughtful about what you put on, and well-tended, you don't have to think about it. Have you ever noticed young girls who constantly tug at their bra straps, pull their skirts down, fuss with their hair? They lack confidence. They have not put in all the work to get to where they want to go. Perfection takes practice. You need to have some experience. Remember that high school friend that never wore heels until the prom came around? She nearly broke her ankle merely walking into the prom.

Didn't you feel sorry for her? She looked absolutely goofy. Women who tell me they can't wear heels (sans a physical condition) haven't practiced. For some reason they missed that developmental phase.

I had a lapse in self confidence (a.k.a., Wallflower Moment) when I walked into the incredibly chic and legendary restaurant Le Bernadin in NYC. I was with my BFF, Zang Toi, the famous designer and illustrator of this book, and his stunning muse. Zang Toi always garners attention because he is, first of all, absolutely adorable beyond belief, and secondly because he is usually wearing a kilt. A very short, luxurious kilt mind you. So the muse also happened to be a famous model at least 6' tall who was wearing one of his drop-dead gowns. Heads turned. EVERY head in the restaurant turned in their direction. It was humbling – like being in the presence of Jesus and Mary, I imagine. That evening I was Jane, Plain Jane, or one of the lambs hanging out at the manger.

So those things happen, and you need to learn to shake it off. What is key is to establish your own personalized, signature look. I know someone who only wears red lipstick – it is the most gorgeous shade against her pearly white skin. It is unforgettable. She has defined her look well, and this is like the cherry on the sundae. She is not perfect, however, you look past that because she is confident and it radiates.

Someone else I know has a unique collection of hats for all occasions. She has thin, curly hair, so she has figured out a way to turn a negative into a positive. Play up your positive assets. If it is your hair, make sure it is fabulous, always. If it is your eyes, don't hide them behind glasses (think Sarah Palin) rather, show them off. And if something works for you, then by all means wear it every day.

I love to wear "evening" fabrics for day. I may throw on a pair of velvet jeans with a cashmere jacket, or a rhinestone belt with a gray flannel dress. This puts a little zing and zip into my day. It is often the surprise element that makes an outfit go from forgettable to memorable. Limit this to one piece only – a little sparkle or shine goes a long way. This can be one of your signature looks. It is one of the many ways you can make something your own. Juxtapose a crisp tailored white shirt (every woman needs at least one) with a lace skirt. Try a ruffled blouse with a pair of classic menswear trousers.

Masculine/Feminine, Ying/Yang, Positive/Negative, Hard/ Soft, opposites attract. This is a great look for a work party or a "meet the parents," when you want to look smart and pulled-together but sexy and sweet, too.

Choose one statement piece and dress around that. It might be a fantastic handbag, a gorgeous top, whatever it is, that is the focal point and everything else becomes secondary. So once you have established your look, say, glamour girl, then you can experiment with toning it down into a more classic look, or moving forward into something trendier. You'll see how easy it is to create your own distinct individual look that is right for your body and personality, and you will be able to customize it to your mood or for an occasion. Get the basic look down, and once you have it figured out, shake it up a bit by adding one unexpected personal touch.

When you look good, you feel good. When you feel good then you can relax and focus your energy on bigger and better things.

Inspiration

For me, nothing beats lady-like, sophisticated glamour. Probably because I loved my mother so much and thought she was the chicest, smartest, most glamorous woman alive. I still have some of her pieces from the 50's that I absolutely treasure. Unfortunately, her waist was about 4 inches smaller than mine is now but I love to look at them occasionally and think of her wearing them. She was loving, compassionate, charitable, confident, professional, bright and efficient. She gave so much of herself, but still took very good care of herself. She had standards. She had expectations of herself, and she was fulfilled and happy. That is how I remember her, and that is who I have modeled myself after, and what I continually strive for.

Look to someone you know. It is important to find a role model, both professionally and personally. It can be several people who possess traits that you admire, as rarely will you like everything about one person. It can be their personality, their intelligence, compassion or strength, for example that you hold in high regard. You might admire one person for a particular quality, and someone else for another. You can look to the style of one and the heart and soul of another. Then begin emulating that quality. Admire people for the right reasons. It is the genuine and best you that you are interested in, after all.

Celebrity style role models abound. Popular choices from the past include Audrey Hepburn, Jackie Onassis, Grace Kelly and Princess Diana. These women have all had incredible "careers" and glamorous international lifestyles. We admire them for their impeccable grooming and classic style savvy. They aged gracefully before our very eyes. They didn't need fake boobs, lips, or lipo-sucked tummies, oh no. Style icons accept the fact that aging is a part of life and embrace it. Current style icons include the "Ashley twins," Gwyneth Paltrow, Sarah Jessica Parker, Reese Witherspoon, Victoria Beckham and Beyoncé to name just a few. There are also many models who set trends, like Kate Moss. What do all these women have in common? They look like they mean it.

Study the person you want to emulate, and I don't mean in a stalking, geeky kind of way. As an example, say you want to have the incredible posture of a colleague. Begin visualizing yourself with that same posture. Study your posture in the mirror, and then adjust yourself so you have it. Jane Fonda looks incredible at her age partly because of her posture. She looks at least 15 years younger than her peers who are slumping due to the natural pull of gravity. Fight it, baby! Become a student of posture. Imbed the positive picture of your ideal posture in your brain. Lock it in. Practice it, live it, believe it. Remind yourself constantly that you can do it. Put post-its on your mirrors or whatever helps you think of it often. You have to begin and believe in order to get. Simple. It will seem uncomfortable at first, but pretty soon it will become second nature. Don't hold yourself back from believing in yourself. You can be anything you want to be, so if a confident posture is part of it, go baby go.

You may, however, be one of those rare originals. Only you know how sure of yourself you are and if you beat to a different drummer. If you indeed, have that figured out already, then good for you. Own it. Fashion is a form of self-expression, so whether you are quiet or loud about it, there is room for everyone. Just err on the side of tastefulness.

Women can easily lose track of themselves as they look after their family. Husbands, lovers, children, parents, friends, pets, they all depend on us for so many things. We barely have time to think straight, let alone stand up straight. But now is the time to start taking care of yourself, for all of their sake, if not your own. Start with something simple like a new haircut. Cut a photo you love out of a magazine and take it into the hair salon with you. It helps if the face shape and texture of the hair are similar to your own. A qualified stylist will help you determine if it is the right cut/color for you. It may take a little time to get used to, but know your hair will always grow if you don't like it. Or wear a hat.

Start exercising. You may find it helpful to do this with a friend. Eat healthier, become more efficient and incorporate lifestyle changes into your regular routine to benefit the whole family. Clean your closet, rethink what works and what doesn't. Make a shopping list and go shopping. Have a complimentary makeover, get a pedicure, don't just sit there, do something. You deserve it. Take the first step and the rest will follow. Besides, by becoming your very best you, you will ultimately inspire others to do the same. If she can do it, I can, too. So look good and be nice at the same time. Wear a smile on your face and live.

Style Definitions

Classic

Bohemian/Hippie Chic

Eclectic

Minimalist

Glamour Girl

Trendy

Girly

Masculine/Feminine

Punk/Gothic

School Girl/Ingénue

Classic

Slim pencil skirt; cashmere twin set; bare legs; classic pumps; hair pulled back into a low ponytail or chignon; clutch; pearl or diamond stud earrings; minimal jewelry; clean, natural-looking makeup

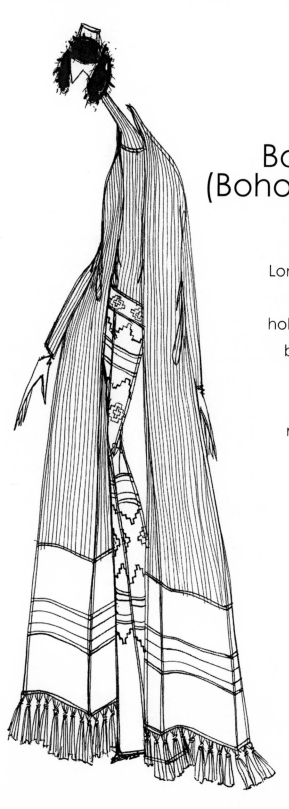

Bohemian (Boho)/Hippie Chic

Long, fringed scarf; bell bottoms; hobo or messenger bag; flat sandals. Hoop earrings; hair au naturel; minimal makeup

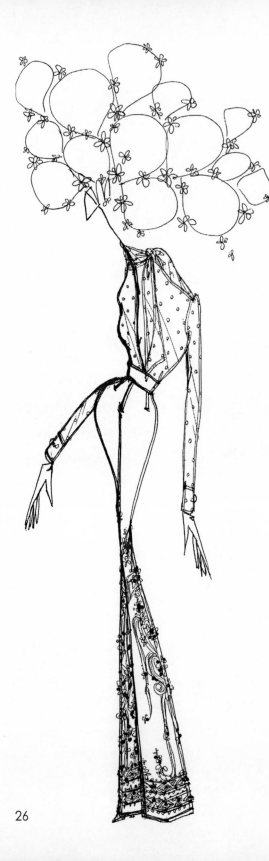

Eclectic

Mixed patterns;
nothing matches
intentionally. Think of
dressing in the dark.

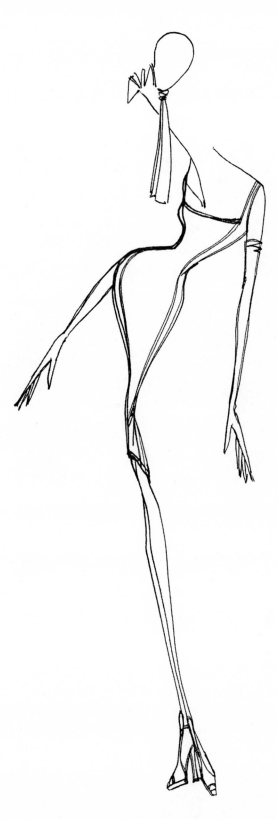

Minimalist

Black, architecturally cut slim pant and jacket with a simple black or white t-shirt. Geometric, straight, blunt-cut hair and a bold, simple, silver cuff. Nothing superfluous.

Glamour Girl

Fur trims, brocade, teetering high heels and designer handbag. Big diamonds; big hair and well-groomed. Everything about her enters the room before she actually does.

Trendy

Whatever is fresh off the runway and the most significant trends worn all at once. This look borders on FASHION VICTIM. It is a meant-to-be-noticed look, and varies from fashion season to fashion season.

Girly

Eyelet; smocking;
ruffled, full-skirted mini
dress. Think flowers,
ribbons, bows, lace
and frills in sugary,
sweet colors. Pretty,
pastel makeup.

Masculine/
Feminine

Balance a tailored
menswear piece or
fabric with something
equally feminine.
A tailored jacket;
white, crisp, ruffled
shirt; high-waisted
trouser; fedora hat
and high-heeled
boots.

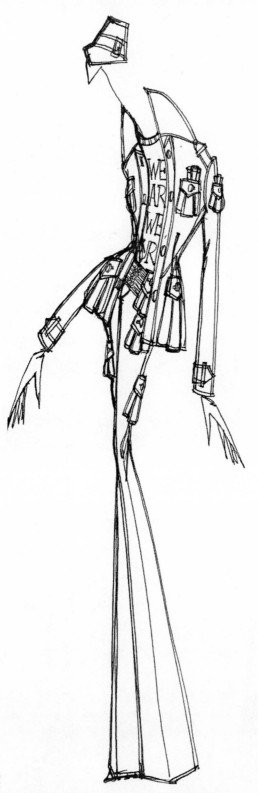

Punk/Goth

Ripped, tight denim; belts with spikes or bullets. Combat boots are essential, plus a leather jacket accessorized with slogans, graffiti, safety pins, razor blades and chains. Dyed and shaved Mohawk and heavy, dark make-up.

School girl/
Ingénue

Plaid, pleated short
skirt; cardigans,
and ballet flats.
Headbands and
ponytails; short,
soft-pink, manicured
nails; fresh and dewy,
clean makeup.

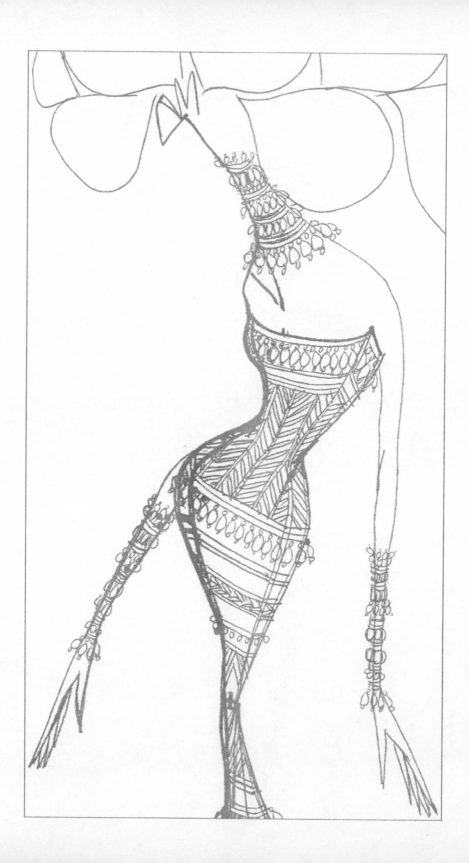

Your Bod

Figure types tend to come in four basic varieties: hourglass, pear, apple or straight. While there are many variations on these themes, this will help guide you generally toward the best fashion choices for your shape.

Hourglass

This figure is curvy-o-rama: larger, full breasts, small waist, full hips and derrière. You should emphasize the waist, as you'll wear belts easily unless you are short-waisted, then a narrower belt or none at all. Wrapped waists and any emphasis on the waist will enhance your curves. Go easy on the cleavage and thigh-high skirt. Choose one part to draw attention to, not all at the same time, or you risk looking like a streetwalker.

Pear

Defined by being small on top – shoulders and bust – and carries her weight on her hips. The secret here is to broaden the shoulder line, bring attention up toward the face and away from the hips. Wear a trench coat with epaulets, shirts and jackets with collars, ruffles, anything with shoulder emphasis or neckline interest that adds volume to the top. Keep the bottom narrower – not tight, just closer to your body. This is not the place to add volume. Darker colors work best on the bottom, lighter on top. A-line skirts help detract from wide hips. Bigger, fuller hair works better than a close-to-the-head "do."

Apple

You're easy to clothe and can wear almost anything. Strong shoulders, a narrow waist and hip line define your figure. Narrow tops and a-line or full skirts create a curvier look, as well as waist emphasis. A wider belt looks great if you have a long waist. If you have swimmer's shoulders, steer clear of shoulder emphasis or details like a jacket with a pointed notch collar that would draw the eye outward.

Straight

This is a boyish figure, with little definition between the bust, waist and hip. The right styles help create a curvier look. Choose pieces with strong shoulders or neckline interest, as well as pieces with weight on the bottom.

A belted safari jacket with cargo pants or a slim skirt with pockets, for example. Sometimes the weight is in the details not the just the cut or shape. Patterns and prints help create interest, too, so go as bold as you want.

Fit and Proportion

There are several variations on the theme. This is why it is so difficult to get the proportion right. There are some looks you just can't wear. If your legs are too short in proportion to your body, for example, don't wear cropped pants or rolled-up jeans. Granted, you can balance the look with a short top and a higher heel, but get serious, it chops off the long, lean leg line. Think monochromatic, narrow and long with a high heel. Don't get choppy! Balance the proportion, with a lean, longer top. You need to experiment: try it on with various shoe heights and see what looks best. Someone else's eye will be drawn to wherever something ends or there is a color break. Why do you think Elizabeth Taylor wears her signature caftans and phenomenal jewelry? She is drawing your eye upward, away from her body and towards those amazing eyes that reflect the jewels. Maximize your assets and minimize the deficits.

The one time vertical can work is when you have a tummy pooch. Ruching across the hips is a good camouflage. Monochromatic always gives you a longer, leaner line. Break up the colors and your eye is interrupted. A slim leg line is best, not flares, or full trousers. NARROW, elongate, bring the eye up or down, not across. Vertical, not horizontal – get the picture? Now, if you are one of fortunate few "inverted" figure types who are tall and thin, you can wear almost anything. Note, I said almost. A cropped top and cropped pants combo is really scary. You will look like you went through the dryer and shrunk. When you wear a jacket that stops right at the hip – your widest point – just shake your head NO. Anywhere you stop the eye had better be what you want to accentuate. A break in the line draws the eye outward, horizontal, wider ...

Follow these general shape guidelines:
- narrow top/fuller bottom
- fuller top/narrow bottom
- full top/full bottom with waist definition
- narrow top/narrow bottom

If your waist is your best feature, belt it or cinch it to make eyes go there first. Don't let the belt rest on your hips. Raise it ¼" higher and the effect is more flattering. Don't cinch it too tightly. Fat will just ooze over it, so it's best to loosen the belt slightly for a smoother look. If your bust is your best feature, then show a little cleavage and no one will ever notice your hips, thighs, big calves, or whatever. Get the picture? Just don't overdo it, showing too much of that cleavage can be vulgar and inappropriate. A tease is much better than the show.

If you have fat ankles, otherwise known as "cankles," or thick calves, do not wear shoes with ankle straps. Do not wear Capri pants, or a mid-calf skirt. Promise me. Hide them. Draw attention away from them, up to your face. Really, I'm sorry, but someone's got to say it. There are specific exercises that can help this area, like squats, I believe, so get busy.

Martha Stewart has a casual chic look that works for her. Sometimes too casual for television, but let's face it, she keeps bees, chickens, dogs and horses. Besides, anyone who does crafts needs washables. Anyway, once she was wearing a sweater with buttons down the front and guess what? It was gapping at the bust. It must have been Cupcake Week on the show.

The point is this is not a good look. It means the sweater is too tight and your clothes just don't fit correctly. I will give Martha credit, though, for being true to her waspy look, and it works for her. She generally looks terrific.

Another faux pas is when your bra is too tight and back fat oozes up over the back strap, i.e., distasteful back cleavage is created. Knits can be forgiving or crucifying, depending on the content and weave as well as the fit. Knitwear and too tight underwear do not make a match. You may be able to have your dry cleaner block the knit to get another inch or so out of a specific area like the bust. Another solution is to try a different bra as this can affect the fit dramatically. So you see why it is so important to try clothes on, move, sit, bend over in them and look at the front and back view. If you see anything scary, don't buy it. Maintain a no-lump strategy.

The shoulder seam of a garment should fit to the outside of the shoulder bone. If you have narrow shoulders, a shoulder pad might be necessary to get the garment to hang correctly. An armhole should not be too deep on something sleeveless to expose a bra. The armhole should lay flat and not gape. The collar should lie flat around the neck, and if a shirt, should button up snugly on the neck.

One of my many most embarrassing moments was when I was a high school cheerleader. We went to the state tournament for basketball that year. Of course we wanted new uniforms. They were jumpers, with side slits and shorts underneath. Underneath that there were knit full bodysuits, so hot, what were we thinking? Sexy I think, but anyway, there we were, doing our opening routine to "The Stripper." I thought I was all that and more, just doing a fabulous job, until the front row of football players began pointing to me and laughing. My first thought was that I was bleeding. Then, I felt it. My shorts were sliding down my legs. By the time I realized what was happening, they were down around my ankles. Mortifying! I ran off the court, half crying and half laughing. My mother was already there to meet me with two large safety pins to secure the elastic in the waist. I still blush when I think of it.

Fabrications

The distinction I want to make here is that whatever you buy, it needs to be the best quality you can afford. Something of quality generally lasts longer, looks and feels better, too. Besides, when you are enveloped in quality fabrics and workmanship it becomes you and it feels fabulous.

Keep in mind, though, that oftentimes, the most expensive and luxurious fabrics are not necessarily the most durable. Silk, chiffon, silk velvet, laces, beaded pieces, are all very fragile. Perhaps a wool flannel pant and a cashmere sweater will do the trick. Some fabrics have more longevity than others. One of the most versatile fabrics is wool gabardine. In a medium weight it works in all but the hottest and coldest days of the year. Just be sure to use a pressing cloth when ironing it so it doesn't get shiny. Dry clean only when absolutely necessary and garments in wool gabardine will last for years.

I also love wool flannel (the poor girl's cashmere) for winter. The higher the quality the softer the "hand" will be. If it feels itchy against your skin, you can layer it. Something in wool crêpe will go a little dressier, and a doubleface wool stretch fabric, jerseys and knits are by far the best travel fabric. Cottons are the best fabric for summer, and cotton poplin is particularly easy care, cool, comfortable and sharp. Cotton knits are easy care too and hold up well. Linen is a luxury fabric, and requires a lot more care, but if wrinkles don't bother you, it is the most comfortable fabric in the heat. I actually sleep in linen sheets all year around. Linen becomes incredibly soft over time.

100% of anything might seem like the most covetable, but it can be more expensive and not necessarily better. An enhanced fabric might have a little Lycra® added for stretch or nylon added for durability. This can be a very good thing. Lycra® is especially great in pants, as it provides stretch for a smooth fit and added comfort. Feel the fabric, try it on, pay attention to its behavior once you get it home and start wearing it. Experience speaks volumes, but it is only worth what you pay attention to.

Prada elevated nylon to a whole new dimension. Not only can nylon be slick, and chic, it is also water resistant and easily packable. Technical fabrics for sports have evolved tremendously and serve very specific purposes.

Cashmere is a no-brainer. I love it. It breathes, is incredibly soft, and cozy. Cashmere comes in a wide variety of quality. Generally, cashmere from Italy is the most covetable, while cashmere from China is of lesser quality. Also, there are various thicknesses of the yarn, referred to as "plys." A good rule of thumb is the larger the number – 6- or 8-ply for example – the thicker and heavier the weight, and the more expensive, warm and luxurious. A 2-ply is nice for spring and summer, or a lighter weight silk/cashmere blend. If 100% cashmere is out of the question, then find a wool and cashmere blend or merino wool.

Knits include cashmere, wool, silk, cotton, linen, and synthetics such as acrylic (ewww) "poly and ester" and other words I can't pronounce or spell. Suffice to say, natural fibers are best. Often, a small percentage of polyester or nylon (for durability) or Lycra® (for stretch) is added to the knit and that is just fine.

Wovens can be made up in all the same fibers as mentioned above in knitwear. So there is the fiber itself; cashmere, cotton, linen, for example, and there is the process of being a knit or a woven. An example of a woven is gabardine (the fabric) made out of wool (the fiber). Another is a shirt, woven in cotton (the fiber) poplin (the fabric). So the cashmere fiber can be a knit or a woven, as in the case of a cashmere pant.

Know that natural fibers breathe. Synthetics trap the heat and become a sauna. A good rule of thumb with natural fabrics is to think how your own skin would respond in that same environment. For example, if you get wet, you dry off with a towel, not in the dryer. The same goes for a sweater. Just lay it flat on a towel to dry.

Knits are a good choice; not only for travel, but for comfort and a wrinkle-free look. If you choose to wear knits, which are warm, comfortable, pack-able, and relatively easy care, pay attention to your lingerie (remember that no-lump strategy).

The fabrications you gravitate to will largely depend on the climate you are in. Heavier wools and cashmere work better in cool climates, while cottons and linens are best in warmer climates. Because we all travel, stores offer many items that provide versatility when traveling amongst a variety of climates.

Remember that a fabric will come in a large variety of quality, so just because something is cashmere, doesn't necessarily conclude that it is a quality garment. Trust your senses to help you determine its value, besides the price tag. In other words, feel it, look at it, even smell it. Leather should smell like leather, not like a synthetic.

Quality over Quantity

You don't need a lot of pieces, just a few good ones. How many times have you gone into your closet of a million pieces, and not been able to find anything to wear? Heartbreaking. Tear jerking and foot stomping probably. If you follow your inspiration and define your look, it will be much easier to find something to wear. Develop a wish list, make a plan and stick to it as much as possible. Be disciplined when it comes to making purchases. It is fun to shop and search for that perfect piece. Once you find it, it is OK to put something on hold and think about it overnight. This helps prevent excessive buying. It is fun to shop; yet buying is another thing entirely. You don't need a lot of stuff. Too much just creates a lot of work, guilt and frustration, and have I mentioned debt? Your wardrobe should be efficient. You need one perfect little black dress, not five. Wait to buy until you find just what you are looking for.

In other words, buy one great piece or outfit if you can afford it each season, take good care of it and add to it every season. Pick a color scheme that you love. Dark colors are the most slimming, so choose one dark color as a base, and then one lighter color to compliment it. For me it's black and white. Both colors look good against my face, they are neutral enough that I never tire of them and I can always accent with any color. Start with two colors and add a third and fourth as accents. So, for example, if you start with gray and ivory, add beige then black, and all four colors work together to make a sophisticated, interchangeable palate with numerous possibilities. Throw in a bright colored accessory as an accent if you want. Believe in it and believe in yourself. Eventually you will have a wardrobe of pieces that work for you. At first you may feel like you need everything, but use restraint. I tend to the classics because I don't tire of them and I consider these investment purchases. If I have the urge to buy a trendier piece, I do it in a fun color and do not spend nearly as much on it as I would a classic piece. You may tire of it after one season, and no one can afford to make expensive fashion mistakes. My guess is you can't either. If you love color, add it into your wardrobe in more inexpensive pieces, like a scarf, shoes, hat, or handbag to pop the look. Eventually you can buy that awesome leather jacket. Brick by brick, build a wardrobe of quality and lasting integrity.

Once you have established a functioning wardrobe that suits you well, conveys your style and meets your "what to wear" needs, you don't stop here. Maintaining your wardrobe is an ongoing process. Replace the basics that you love and that show signs of wear, and update with a few new seasonal pieces to keep you current and a skip in your step. The good news is you don't have to keep starting over every season. You should be able to budget for your seasonal clothing expenditures and stick to it. This includes both basic replacements, and a few "of the season" items.

Remember it takes years to get to the point sans frustration, when you open your closet doors to your really best friends, your clothes. When you think, "I haven't worn you in so long, I can't wait until ... the weather warms up, I have the right occasion, or I lose a few pounds. Hello, girlfriend, it's good to see you again. That is nearly wardrobe nirvana.

General color combination guideline:

dark base	light	complimentary	accent
gray	ivory	camel	black
chocolate	yellow	lime green	orange
chocolate	beige	ivory	blue/pale pink
navy	white	red	yellow
black	white	fuchsia	orange
black	white	turquoise	jade green
wine	ivory	olive green	camel

Dressing Appropriately

Punctuate the moment – dress appropriately and deliberately for each and every occasion. This means not wearing a bikini to a wedding, a dress to the beach and yoga pants for anything but yoga. Now obviously there are many variations on the theme, which helps us all to express ourselves in our own unique fashion. What do you want to say? Do you want to be the butt of the joke that everyone talks about afterwards? That's fine, but if so, go for it and do it really well, make it memorable – dramatic, over the top. On the other hand, if you do not want to be singled out, be a sheep – whisper. Dress in a socially appropriate way so you fit in and will not be particularly observed. There is a lot of space in the middle for your personal signature, and that is the intention.

We will remember what we wear to a special occasion. I will never forget my First Holy Communion dress and veil. I remember the smell, how the fabric felt against my skin and better yet, how it made me feel. I felt very special, holy as a matter of fact. I actually said to myself, "I will remember this day for the rest of my life." Important occasions call for important dress. We have our photos taken and albums are made, as well as resulting memories. You'll remember when you wore ...

Charity or Bridal luncheon – A "pretty" suit or dress. Think ladylike. A hat may or may not be acceptable depending on the city/location. Leave the work tote in the car, and opt for a small clutch or handle bag. There is rarely room at the table for much more. Park it under your seat, btw.

Sporting event – Casual but put together, perhaps a skinny pant and twin set with ballet flats or a well fitting jean, shirt and sweater or casual jacket. Cute sneakers are OK unless you are in a box seat, and then dress it up a bit by changing your shoes and leaving the baseball cap at home. Definitely pants, though, no skirts or dresses as you may have to climb stairs or people may have to crawl past you in the seat. And promise me you won't wear the team colors unless you are actually attending that college.

Grocery Shopping – You can wear the same casual attire as above, but please, look put-together, like you care about yourself.

Wedding – The invitation should provide you with the correct information to determine what to wear. See the "Evening" section for further explanation.

When in Doubt, Pull It Out

Wardrobe essentials/must haves!

- little black dress
- gabardine suit
- fabulous-fitting jean
- crisp white shirt
- cashmere twin set
- sundress or shirtdress
- trench coat
- animal-print something

little black dress. Something that looks terrific on you, and that makes you feel fabulous. For years mine has been a black sheath (usually Chanel) in a lightweight wool crepe. It is seasonless, goes from day to evening, lunch to dinner to a cocktail party, depending on how I accessorize it. For day, tie a cardigan over your shoulders; wear black lizard pumps (I love animal-skin shoes – they are ever-so-chic and can last forever). Carry a mid-sized bag that you can put enough into, but isn't as big and clunky as a tote. Then tie a silk scarf around your neck, add some big black shades, and channel Audrey Hepburn or Jackie O. Another option is pearl earrings and a pearl choker – so classic. You can go from a business meeting to dinner in this look. For a cocktail party or if you want to make it dressier, add a silver metallic shoe and small clutch and a shawl or satin trench coat.

gabardine suit.
Preferably in black, navy, or charcoal. Well-tailored, perfectly proportioned for your figure, you go girl. Again, this will take you anywhere you need to go. For a luncheon or the office, I love it paired with a crisp white shirt, preferably with French cuffs and a spread collar that is neither too small nor too large – just right. Always "pop" the collar. The same accessories work as for the little black dress, but for a dressier evening, switch out the white blouse for a little beaded or lace top – something that says sexy. The pant should be fabulous fitting, and something you can pair up with almost anything, including your crisp white shirt or twinset, and topped with the trench. Three matching pieces are an ideal base, so if there is a skirt that matches the jacket buy that too. The skirt style should suit your body type, and generally the more classic (straight or a-line) the better and more versatile.

fabulous-fitting jean.
This falls into the same category as a bathing suit. Most of us would rather die than face ourselves in those terribly lit fitting rooms. But, life is full of things we just have to endure. I was hoping never to have to lie on the bed to zip myself in my jeans, but alas, skinny jeans are back. At least now they have stretch in them. Pair the jean with a skinny knit if you are skinny, or a sexy slightly sheer tunic top if you are not, or a crisp white shirt. Add a jacket as the anchor; don't forget the exclamation point – a high-heeled boot or sandal depending on the weather, and voila!

crisp white shirt.
Made of cotton or linen, it should fit great, and be the thing you throw on all the time to feel good. I love one with French cuffs, and I like mine fitted with a bit of Lycra®. Wash this, and if it has Lycra®, line dry it, and it will retain its fresh color. A big artist's-style shirt is great

too – you can belt it if you want, or wear it loose with leggings or a narrow leg and flats. When you find the perfect shirt, buy several. You won't regret it.

cashmere twin set.
A cardigan acts as a jacket, you can tie it around your waist or shoulders, and it takes up little room if you stuff it in your bag! The underpinning can be any shape be it a turtleneck, t-shirt, or a shell, for example. You should feel good in the fit, and buy the best quality you can afford. The key here is they match and you can wear them singly or together as a set for an alternative to a jacket.

sundress or shirtdress.
A summer essential look is a great sundress or shirtdress. If you like a more feminine look, something white and crocheted, eyelet and tiered, or a pretty pastel colored baby doll shape can be so forgiving. I love a classic halter dress, strapless simple a-line (flattering for most everyone) or shirtdress (especially good if you are busty or want to be more modest) in crisp poplin, in white, khaki or black. I keep my accessories minimal, assuming it is hot outdoors. Some great bangles and cute sandals and don't forget the fabulous sunglasses and summer handbag and you are good to go.

trench coat.
This has become an alternative for a jacket. Choose a classic neutral color or a fabulous green, red, orange or yellow – something fun to give your wardrobe some punch. A short trench is an alternative to a suit jacket. Something about a trench just says you are there, it is a bit of a power look, and significant without trying too hard.

animal-print something.
These include leopard, cheetah, zebra, Dalmatian, and more. Animal prints pack a punch, so pair them with solids. One wild animal goes a long way, so resist the temptation to wear it head-to-toe.

The Goods

Jeans and pants

Everyone must have several great fitting pair of jeans.

They are as basic as water and moisturizer. One often must try on hundreds of jeans to find the right pair. Don't you hate it when there is a hot jean and you just have to have them to be hip and cool even if they look terrible on you? Your friends won't say so; they don't want to hurt your feelings, but they are all thinking the same thing. Walk behind her so no one sees her bottom in those jeans. That is a BFF for sure.

The derrière is the most important part of the jean. This is where everyone looks, whether you notice or not. Look in a three-way mirror.

Make sure the jeans fit your most difficult area first. If your hips are the toughest part to fit, find a jean that fits there first. You can alter the leg, hem, and waist. If you have an ample derriere, choose a style without pockets. The seaming should draw your eye down, as should a yoke. (That's no yoke!) Buy a jean with a back yoke always – unless you have a perfect, small, tight, high bottom.

If you have a flat derrière, look to a yoke plus pockets with flaps or some detail to add something extra. If the rise (the length between the top of the pant and the crotch) is too short, it will ride up your crack, and if it is too long, will bag like you pooped your pants. Neither is desirable.

For large thighs, do not under any circumstances choose a jean with cargo pockets or added detail. Less is best. Denim will stretch as you wear it, but don't fit them so tightly that it causes the extra inches to create a muffin top. Choose darker denim for a dressier look, and a bleached or a washed jean for the weekend. If the jean fits well, and you love it, buy more than one pair. I love a jean with stretch. Stretch will give you a super sexy fit, hugging your curves, besides being comfortable. Wear them as long as you can. An inch off the ground is the rule. They shouldn't drag on the ground, as they will fray, get wet, and look sloppy. But wear them long so you get a more elongated look. Try them on with whichever shoe or heel height you prefer. You can usually get by with the same length for a flat and kitten heel, but not a 4" heel. Skip the trend of big-cuffed jeans. It only shortens your legs and makes you look stumpy. Opt for a fluid menswear trouser with a gentle cuff; it can look fantastic given the correct proportion. The shorter legged you are, the slimmer the leg silhouette and the cleaner or less embellished they should be. A really full pant will drag you down. Those work best with a small, accentuated waist and smaller, tighter fitting top. A boot-cut pant balances out fuller hips, as it helps create a long slim line. This is the reason a skinny pant doesn't work and creates a lollipop effect. The straighter and skinnier you are the more of a low rise you can wear. Boyish figures are the only ones who can pull this look off well. If you have a tummy, and slim legs, choose a style that has some stretch to hold in your stomach, hits just blow the belly button, and a straight style leg to accentuate your assets. This is why finding the correct fit is work, but well worth the effort.

Denim stretches with wear, and fades with washing. Either dry clean them or hang dry them to maintain the color. Do put them in the dryer on low heat for 10-15 minutes after hang drying to soften them and pull them back into shape.

If you wear hose or tights keep the waistband of the hose hidden beneath the waistband of the pants. If you are wearing low rise pants, wear a most minimal thong to keep your panties from peeking out. Avoid "camel toes," when your pants are too short in the rise, and by all means don't wear anything with a seam that slices you vertically.

Shorts

Shorts aren't for everyone. Short shorts should only be worn by the young, and firm, and then only if you have great legs. If you have varicose veins, flab or wrinkles on your knees, choose a Capri pant or knee length skirt as a good substitute for warm weather. I wonder if Botox can be injected in those wrinkles. Other people don't want to see that stuff so keep it hidden. A fuller skort will make your legs look thinner but most importantly the length is critical. Pay attention to wear the short ends, as it is most flattering when it hits at the thinnest part of your leg. A cropped pant looks best resting just above the anklebone or where the shin indents.

Skirts

Same idea here, wear those short skirts if you are young and/or have great legs, Skirts are a wonderful alternative to pants and often more comfortable and flattering. Pay attention to your proportion when pairing the top half of the equation. Straight slim skirts and fuller skirts are a little harder to work with. If you are hippy, then don't wear these extreme shapes. An a-line is the all around best choice for ease, and workability. Length is perhaps the biggest factor in getting a skirt of any shape to look right. Just above the knee or just below the knee is better than in the middle of the knee. The eye will be attracted to where the skirt ends, and knees aren't that good to look at. If you have ugly knees, and there are plenty out there, cover them. So proportion of the top with the bottom, and the correct length for that proportion on your proportions are critical. You can't just throw on any top with any skirt and expect it to be good to go. Become a student of your figure and figure it out. Don't be tempted to roll your skirt up if it is too long. I already tried that with my pleated uniform skirt in 7th grade. It was uneven and lumpy then, and would be today, too.

Underpinnings

This is a good place to save money. Camisoles, t-shirts, novelty tops all peak out from under a jacket or cardigan. It should feel good against your skin. The neckline should lay well with whatever you have over it. My most favorite thing is a cozy turtleneck in the cold weather and a cotton camisole or basic crew neck t-shirt or polo shirt in the summer. Watch the sales, you can purchase them in several colors to give your outfit that POP!

An underpinning becomes an outer "top" when it looks good enough to stand on its' own. Tunics, peasant tops, a gorgeous camisole, anything made of a beautiful fabric or that carries interesting detail works.

If tucking in your shirt, tuck it into your hose for a smooth line and to help keep it tucked in. Reach under your skirt if you are not wearing hose and pull the top down firmly.

Jackets/Suits

The mismatched "suit" is a more updated, casual look for everyday office wear. Nothing beats a well-fitting jacket. Pair it with a contrasting skirt for warm weather, and a pant for cooler weather. The shape of the jacket will dictate the shape of the skirt. For example, a shorter, fitted jacket works best with a full skirt or full-legged pant. A short boxy jacket works best with a straighter skirt, short or long. A longer boxy jacket needs a slim pant, while a long and lean jacket works best over a slim pant or skirt. These are basic guidelines, there are many variations on the theme, but if you stick to this in general you will be fine.

Coats

Coats have oomph. They are substantial, and can represent a significant share of your clothing budget. There are dress coats, parkas, ponchos, raincoats and more. Fabrics include wool, alpaca, cashmere, nylon to name just a few, besides leather and fur (real or faux). You need several coats to cover various types of occasions. To start, choose a great fitting cloth coat in tweed or solid that can be paired with a dress for dinner, then take you all the way with jeans and a sweater for Saturdays. A short jacket like a pea coat or ¾-length leather jacket will become an everyday acquaintance. Depending on climate, choose weights that work for you. A thin nylon jacket is lightweight and easy to tote around. Sports and outdoor activities will determine what else you need more specifically. Choose a coat with a raglan sleeve if you need to wear it over a suit jacket. This will give you more room to move and you won't risk ripping out the armhole seams. Take your time and make a careful decision about a coat purchase. You'll own it for years.

Dresses

A beautiful dress can certainly make a girl feel special. Sundresses, day dresses, cocktail dresses, shifts, shirtdresses, sheaths, something in all shapes and for all occasions. A dress doesn't give you as much mileage as a separate item like a skirt, pant or shirt. What a dress does do for you though, is give you a finished, already put together look. You have to love the way the dress looks and feels first and foremost.

Evening

Evening is a world of its own. There are evening bags, evening shoes, evening makeup and evening hair. A special blow out or up do says you made an effort and this is a special night. The day of an event you should book your manicure, pedicure, hair and makeup application if need be. Do not under any circumstances book a facial a week or less before an important event. Yikes – in case you haven't heard, you breakout typically after a facial! Better not to use a handbag at all (boyfriends and husbands are usually willing to carry a lipstick in their pocket – it's sexy), than use a day bag – too big and just the wrong look. Evening is more delicate, special, thought out. Also, a little sparkle goes a long way.

My recommendation is to buy a black silk sheath, and buy the best quality you can afford (years ago I absolutely wore out a Dior signature print silk chemise that I am still sick I can't replace!) Pair that with Manolo Blahnik or Jimmy Choo strappy peau de soi or metallic sandals. Add a small clutch, pearl or diamond earrings, a pashmina or cashmere shawl or black cashmere cardigan and you can go just about anywhere, other than a black-tie affair.

There are gowns and then there are gowns. If you find yourself attending numerous events, it is worth building a gown wardrobe. Gowns really don't follow trends as quickly as sportswear or ready to wear so a beautiful gown will be wearable 10+ years from now.

A ballgown is the most appropriate for white tie or very formal black tie events. A column gown works for every other black tie occasion, and for many occasions, a dressy cocktail dress works, too. Buy something that looks good on you – accentuates your assets and makes you feel like a million bucks. Try on several pieces with different shapes and necklines. You may be surprised what looks the best on you may not be what you had in mind at all. When in doubt, go to a Carmen Marc Valvo-designed gown. He is the master of the shutter-pleat technique. These gowns look amazing on nearly everyone. He is a designer that truly loves and understands American women of every shape and size and I am one of his biggest fans.

Gowns tend to accentuate the décolletage more often than not, probably because they cover up the legs. Watch the way the bust line and the derrière look particularly. Wear a long line strapless bra unless you have really good boobs. You need the support, and the uplift on the cleavage. And watch the panty lines. Sometimes it is better to go with a more structured gown where the bustier is built in and the garment has "bones" to give you shape.

Leave the form-fitting silk bias cut gowns for the skinny young things (SYTs). Practice waving if you have a sleeveless dress, and if your arm waddles, don't wear it. If you have underarm flab that rises up over a strapless gown (not to be confused with your boob) skip this silhouette, too.

Make an entrance. Start with the walk. Walk the Goddess Walk. Head held high, say, "I know who I am and where I am going, so dream on!" Practice in front of the mirror. Practice walking up and down stairs. Escalators can be treacherous.

It would be rather embarrassing to be doing the goddess walk and trip up the escalator. Many a train has been caught in one of these contraptions. Trains are very difficult to maneuver. When you turn with a train you need to kick the train out with one foot so it creates a sweep behind you. This is perfect for full-length photos. The real issue with trains is that once you master the movement of them, they can easily get caught in an escalator or worse. Some well-intentioned guest, who just happened to miss the fact that your gown followed you for five feet, steps on it and something rips.

I've had this happen more than once and occasionally it has caused the front of my dress to pull down in a rather rapid motion. Spare yourself the embarrassment. If you absolutely must, then there are two more things you should consider. When standing in a crowd and other than for a photograph, pull the train closely into you near your feet, or hold the train with your hand. This means, of course, that you cannot eat, drink, hold your handbag or shake hands very easily. And if there is dancing, have your dressmaker put a small "eye" on the back of the dress at the beginning of the train, near the back of your knee roughly. Then you can simply "hook" the train up to the back of the dress and it becomes the same length all around. Granted, it isn't as dramatic and beautiful, but it works and keeps you and everyone else on the dance floor from tripping on and ruining your gorgeous gown.

If you frequently attend lot of black tie or cocktail parties, keep a file of what you wear where. Keep an index card or photo journal per party – what you wore, what group or event, so you don't repeat yourself. When you are known for your fashion sense particularly, people will look forward to seeing what you'll wear.

If you are invited to an event, the invitation should suggest the appropriate attire. If it doesn't, call and ask your host.

Here are the guidelines:

White Tie means wear a ballgown, elbow gloves, fur, your best jewelry – the works. This is the most formal of occasions.

Black Tie means wear a gown or very dressy cocktail dress.

Cocktail Attire means wear a cocktail dress or evening suit or a dressy pant ensemble.

Festive Attire does not mean wear a themed sweater with the holiday symbols knit into it (how much do I hate that?) It means simply to put something special on, like a red dress for the holidays (those ornament earrings that light up remain in your drawer).

Business Attire means wear a suit or dress that you would wear to a board meeting or business lunch. Nothing too tight or revealing.

Casual Attire means still very put-together and thought out, but perhaps what you would wear shopping or to a museum, not what you would wear to participate in a sporting event.

Dive-In

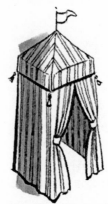

Shopping for a swimsuit is not my favorite thing. There is nothing more frightening than standing in your underwear in a brightly lit fitting room in the middle of winter, looking pasty white, with extra winter weight. Look as cute as you can, for yourself, when you go to try on swimsuits. Shave your legs, make it a good hair day, and put on a little makeup, too. It is tough enough for most of us to look in the poorly lit fitting room mirror. Unless you have a fantastic body, and rarely does anyone think that, think camouflage.

Full-hipped/full derrière

Choose darker bottoms, stay away from big patterns or horizontal stripes. Anything that draws attention towards the hips is wrong. Focus on the top. There should be enough fabric to cover your cheeks. Low riding boy shorts works well.

Slim-hipped

A belted style, boy shorts, horizontal stripes, larger patterns and details like pockets will all add visual weight.

Tummy

A higher-waisted bottom, a maillot with shirring at the waist, a tankini that hits at or below the bottom all work great.

Thick waist

Look for something that will draw the eye into the center of the waist, like a keyhole, a flower, or shirring that focuses the eye there.

No waist

Create the visual effect of a waist, with a belted maillot, with horizontal stripes, or shirring. Draw attention up to the bust if that is your best shot!

Long torso

A top with a wide band underneath the bust helps the eye to shorten the distance between the top and the bottom. Think of reducing the mass of the midsection. A tankini, a higher waisted bottom, horizontal stripes all help to break up the torso.

Short torso

A low cut bottom and a teeny weensy top (think the beaches of Brazil) is best if you can pull it off. The opposite of a long torso, try to create the most space between a top and a bottom, thus creating the illusion of more skin.

Large-busted

A solid color works best, and stays away from everything listed below for small busted. Be sure it is an adequately constructed under-wire top so you have the support you need,

Small-busted

Select styles with under wire, light padding, patterns, shirring or gathering at the center of the bust line. Ruffles or anything that adds some extra fabric to the top will help balance you out.

In my case, I am not big enough for the big girl ones, i.e., Miracle suits that suck all the fat in so it pushes your cleavage up to your neck. Not so lucky. My belly will stick out farther than my boobs in profile. Approach everyone I meet head-on.

No walking along the beach – straight in the surf, sharp turn, and back to beach chair. I am going to practice now, all the while sucking in my stomach muscles (!) until I want to throw up. Nevertheless, finding a cute cover-up or pareo to wear coming and going from the beach or pool is essential.

A positive body image is imperative. We know that being grossly overweight is extremely unhealthy, so of course I am not encouraging that. But when I say positive body image I don't mean the image that others judge as positive. We are not all the same, and very few of us look like the fashion models in the magazines. I mean whatever body image that truly makes you feel good about yourself. Then figure out your best features and maximize them. Don't draw attention or even ever mention your flaws – real or not – ever again.

Icing on the Cake

It is important to look good on the inside, no matter what you are wearing on the outside. My mother always said that you should wear pretty matching underwear in case you are in a car accident. Right. When you wear beautiful lingerie you instantly feel beautiful.

Lingerie

Lingerie should make you feel good. Beautiful, soft cottons, gorgeous French laces, pretty colors. Whatever makes you feel sexy. Granny panties have to go, and there is absolutely no excuse for visible panty lines (VPLs). A panty should fit smoothly, with no bunching or pulling. A little Lycra® or spandex in the fiber content can help. Cotton is imperative for exercising, and always choose a panty, even in lace, with a cotton crotch. Defer to a skin toned nude color under white, even white shows under white. No dark colors under light colored pants or skirts. The secret to a thong is to buy it a size larger than you would a panty. They are uncomfortable when they are too tight. Besides, anything too tight makes your fat spill over and creates the muffin-top effect. Not a good look.

Lingerie is where you might be able to save some money. If you are wearing lingerie for entertainment, the person you are entertaining doesn't really care. It usually comes off pretty fast. So go to Victoria's Secret for all that unless you can really afford La Perla or Eres. If you have particular fit issues, you need to buy good quality with help from an experienced fit specialist. You are wearing the wrong bra if the back band rides up, if your breasts peak out the sides of the cups, and if the straps keep falling off your shoulders.

Breast size changes over a woman's lifetime. Gaining or losing weight, pregnancy, nursing, exercising, aging, can all play a factor in your breast size. It is recommended you get re-fitted for a bra once a year. Bras lose their elasticity with wear and washing. The fit specialist will measure the circumference under and around the fullest part of your bust. Once you know your size, try on a variety of styles until you find the perfect support. Just like with apparel, different manufacturers will fit slightly differently. Lean over to put the bra on so your breasts fall into the cups. Look in a three-way mirror to be sure you like the fit all the way around. The bra should fit best on the middle set of hooks. This will give you a little leeway either way. The right lingerie will help you perfect the look of your breasts in a particular piece of clothing. There are t-shirt bras, strapless pushup bras, and long-line bras. Take the right bra for that particular garment. My bra wardrobe consists of black, nude, white, and pretty fashion colors for fun. I love lace, but it doesn't necessarily look good under most smooth fabrics. No bumps or lumps. The idea of metal in the underwire has been reported to be a medical risk, so I only wear underwire if it improves the look of what I am wearing.

Here is my list of lingerie "must haves"

- Convertible bra in black and nude (strapless, racer back, halter)

- Long-line bra in nude

- Sports bra in white and/or nude

- Padded, push-up bra OR a minimizer in black and nude

- T-shirt bra with smooth cups for just that

Then add an assortment of fashion lingerie with matching thongs, boy shorts, and a nice selection of sexy lingerie of your choice.

What about cleavage? If you are flatter-chested or just average, sometimes a little padding can make the difference between wallflower and knockout. The gel pads are fantastic. They feel like the real thing if you're pressed against someone. They are referred to as cookies, cutlets, boobies, and so on. Be sure they are placed evenly under the breast, and they do not peak out of anywhere – ever. Another secret used by models and film stars is tape. I don't advise this if you have an adhesive allergy, but white medical tape works the best. Put it under your breast and pull up on the side then press on the tape to hold it firmly. This gives you an automatic lift, and won't show under the skimpiest of clothes. Your breast should not be pointing down. Nice round mounds at the top of the dress are desirable. Pushing your breasts up to your chin is not, however, unless you are performing in a Shakespearean play.

Another thing you can do to enhance the cleavage is to use a contour cream to create shadow and light. I recommend utilizing the skills of a makeup artist to teach you how to apply it, as this can get very tricky. Besides, you don't want to get any makeup on your clothes.

Cleavage is never appropriate for business. Save it for the beach, dinner, dating, and ... seduction. Check out the side profile also, so you don't have breasts sagging out the side of a tank top or sundress. Not a good look. A beautiful camisole can be a pretty underpinning if shown as a peek. I actually saw someone at a party recently wearing a black bra with a completely cutout blouse over it, so you really didn't see any of the blouse in front, just the bra. I thought it was a joke, or a costume or something. What happened to the surprise factor? That is when the "If you've got it, flaunt it" axiom backfires. What, if you have "bad taste" flaunt it?

Nipples – depending on you and the occasion, it can be an advantage or disadvantage to show them off! If you choose not to show them off, wear a t-shirt bra, or use small, round Band-aids.

On the flip side of breast enhancement are the minimizer bras. If you have very large breasts stay away from anything too skimpy. There is just no place to hide. A good fitting bra will hide a multitude of sins. Queen Latifah does a tasteful job of displaying her ample breasts so they look shapely, as does Oprah. They certainly know how to work their assets.

Large-breasted women should never ever go braless – not only does it make you sag, it is not pretty. Those sisters need support. If you run, you need a jog bra as bouncing breasts cause sagging. Being fitted in the right bra is a must, and it doesn't cost anything to go to the lingerie department and have a professional fit you.

Choose the right lingerie carefully so straps don't peek out from underneath the clothes you wear. Lingerie straps or "Jenny" straps are a wonderful trick to keep this from occurring. Have your seamstress sew in a small snap under the shoulder strap or on the shoulder seam. Then attach a small piece of fabric across it. Then when you put the dress on, you can snap the bra strap into place and it won't move.

Handbags

Go for a classic designer bag like Chanel, Gucci or Louis Vuitton if you can. It is so worth the investment in terms of sophistication, your fashion statement and timelessness. Don't make this first major purchase too "of the season" or you may regret it. It will always look like that season, and unless you can afford to buy one every season or even every year, resist the temptation. This is a good example of a time you may want to buy a good quality knock-off in the meantime, and save for the classic. You may get lucky and find a gently used designer classic on eBay or in a consignment or vintage shop.

I bought my first Chanel handbag 25 years ago, and I still have it. I wore that bag daily for years, too. I took impeccable care of it though, refurbishing it through Chanel every other year. Since then, I am an admitted designer handbag addict. When you purchase beautiful things of quality, you take better care of it.

A few years ago, I visited one of the factories where the iconic Chanel handbags are made outside of Paris. It was a pilgrimage. Once through the unmarked security gates, there before me stood the cleanest, most orderly and contemporary workplace you can image. I slowly made my way past the design room, where Karl Lagerfeld's sketches for the season loomed. There was a room filled floor to ceiling with small, labeled drawers with the hardware and trims of the handbags in the sketches. There was a temperature controlled room to store the leather hides, and a room where elaborate scientific testing is done to ensure longevity and durability of the bags. I tried to take it all in, including the women in white lab coats expertly braiding the chain straps, the cutters taking knife to hide with painstaking precision, the sewers expertly guiding the machines so the stitching is flawless. It was fascinating, and reinforced my appreciation of the process of expert workmanship.

A high-quality leather handbag has higher-quality construction, so generally is much more durable. The stitching is tighter so the straps don't break, the hardware is attached more securely so they hold longer, and the overall construction and materials are of much higher quality. The lining doesn't rip the first season you have it. It retains its shape if your store it properly, stuffed with tissue and put in its own cloth bag and stored upright on the shelf. Some people like to look at them all and don't store them in the bag, but I don't change my handbag every day, so this way works for me. A fabulous feature on a handbag is "feet" on the bottom of the bag. You can have more freedom for where you set your handbag down. But oftentimes there are hooks under the table or bar of a restaurant, which is handy. Even better, though, was something I discovered at a divine restaurant overlooking the sea on the Amalfi Coast in Italy. It was already a perfectly beautiful day, and I was starry eyed on this romantic trip in the company of my future husband. Just when I thought it couldn't get any better, the waiter carefully placed a special stool for my handbag next to my seat so I could place my white Chanel handbag on it. A pedestal for your "It" bag.

Aside from carrying life's necessities in my handbag, try not to get too carried away. The larger the handbag, the more stuff you carry, and the heavier it is. After a while, this weight can take its toll on your neck and shoulders. Better to carry a tote with a smaller handbag inside. Fill the tote with non-essentials, and put just lipstick, phone, wallet, keys and maybe a compact in your bag. The water, fragrance, makeup, hairbrush, and paperback go into the tote.

I keep a lot of non-necessities in my car instead of my handbag. One of my favorite things to carry in my car is handy wipes. If you go to an office and use a desk, keep it stocked as well. Include healthy snacks so you won't be tempted to visit the vending machine. We schlep too much stuff around. Someone told me I looked like a mule once, carrying a handbag, briefcase, and gym bag all at once. So whatever you can pare down, do. The big totes and hobo bags are difficult to keep organized. Look for a bag with compartments, preferably at least one inside zippered pocket and a cell phone pocket. Then use a small makeup bag for all your makeup. Keep a pencil, pen, and business cards in the zippered compartment. Look for straps that will fit over your shoulder with a coat. The handbag shouldn't hit you right at your hip – have the strap shortened at the same place you have your shoes repaired. When traveling or walking down a city street, wear the shoulder strap across your body if it is long enough to avoid being a target of theft. If it is a handle bag hug it against your body rather than on your wrist or in your hand for the same reason.

When you are purchasing a new handbag take the stuff out of your handbag, and organize it into the new handbag before you actually buy it. Does it work? Then put it on your shoulder and/or in your hand and look in the mirror from all angles. Does it suit your look, your lifestyle, and your body's proportions? A small girl with a huge bag does not work.

For travel, I like to have a handbag with an outside pocket to carry my passport, boarding pass and itinerary to expedite security and boarding when your hands might be holding a latte and another bag or whatever. It should be large enough to accommodate a bottle of water and a magazine, too.

Buy the best handbag you can afford, in classic colored leather. Light colors will soil easily, as well as suede, so I recommend you avoid these for your everyday bag. When you develop a wardrobe of handbags, you can add these on as "luxury items."

Your handbag wardrobe should include a "go-everywhere" tote, an everyday workhorse bag (this would be my first designer bag), a smaller bag that could fit in the tote for travel, and a special, interesting evening bag. Then as you build your wardrobe, you can add a summer bag in straw or fun-colored leather, a new everyday bag, and a smaller clutch for dinner or luncheons.

There are particular bags I don't recommend. As I've said, hobo bags are the most difficult to find things in. The first and last time I used one I found myself emptying out the entire contents on the curb to find my car keys. The doctor bag shape is hard to get into in a rush, and I always scratch myself on the zipper closure. I like an evening bag with a handle that fits over my wrist so I can hold a glass of wine and still shake hands. Wearing a shoulder strap on an evening dress usually compromises the look and "hang" of the dress and can damage a fragile fabric. A clutch can work, too, but takes some practice with a cocktail while shaking hands.

A friend has all of her small inner bags (wallet, key case, makeup bag) in different colors so she can see what is in the bag and retrieves them easily. I happen to like all the pieces inside my handbag to be matching. I know, hard to imagine. You might want to have a bright keychain or phone so they are easier to find. Remember, if you were in an accident, and your handbag went flying all over the place, you would want all the components to match.

I have to say, I still carry a small Louis Vuitton bag I bought 15 years ago. I have replaced the strap several times, and most recently, put their short gold chain strap on it. I use it for a makeup bag inside my larger handbag, but I also still use it when I am traveling and need a dinner bag. It goes with everything, is absolutely invincible, and undeniably one of the best things I have ever bought. It is in that classic LV monogram series (oh, don't ask me how much of that I own, but I bought it all over years and am so glad I did) and it still looks great.

Keep your handbag clean. Take everything out of it and dump it over the trash can. It is amazing how all those paper clips and little bits of paper just appear. Wipe the lining with a slightly damp cloth. Store it properly by stuffing it with tissue paper to retain the shape. If it came with a storage bag, use it. It will prevent it from getting dusty and scratched, so the next time you use it you will be ready to go. If you have a thousand handbags you may want to leave them out of the bags so you can figure out which is which. But for most of us, this is a good way to go. If you keep them colorized on the shelf you can figure it out pretty easily. I keep mine by category; i.e., evening bags together, straw/summer totes together, and so on.

Jewelry

Nothing beats a great piece of jewelry – real, not fake. I suggest first buying a good-quality pair of small diamond studs. Ask your jeweler if you can "trade up" and exchange them down the road for a bigger and better pair. Oftentimes a reputable jeweler will let you do this. If you can't spring for diamonds, then buy a pair of cubic zirconium, or a classic pair of hoops in gold or silver, or pearl studs. All of these styles go anywhere.

There is appropriateness in terms of jewelry as well as in everything else. I mentioned evening jewelry earlier. For day I prefer classic, such as diamonds, pearls, silver or gold. But whatever your preference, your jewelry should be in keeping with your overall look. If you are into boho chic, then long strands of colorful stones, or chandelier earrings, and a more artsy, handmade one of a kind piece would work well. Casual wear usually means less jewelry, but a strand of pearls wrapped ever so casually around the neck paired with a chic black maillot at the beach is simply IT. Beach jewelry is generally more casual and inexpensive though, so think bold, fun, colorful. Wood bangles or a bold turquoise cuff can add that bit of panache. Take direction from your bathing suit style.

Really think of your total look when you are accumulating your jewels. Silver? Gold? Delicate? Heavy? Classic? Bohemian? Less is more, and one important piece is better than a bunch of junk hanging off of you. For example, skip a necklace with a heavy drop earring. Bracelets work if they are of the same weight to balance the earrings. The rule of thumb is take one accessory off after you think you are ready to go. In the words of Mies Van der Rohe, "less is more." Jewelry should enhance what you are wearing unless it is fine (real) jewelry. In that case, choose your clothes to complement the piece(s).

Consider hair ornaments as jewelry, too, so they should relate to the other pieces. Take into account the hardware on your shoes and bag. If you are wearing lots of silver but your shoes or bag have a big gold buckle, it won't work.

Once you start accumulating a quality wardrobe of well thought out meaningful pieces you'll find you can occasionally sneak in something faux. Your eye will begin to spot quality and the more you familiarize yourself with it the more discerning you will become. Coco Chanel had her real pieces copied and then wore the copies; hence the popularity of costume jewelry had begun. If you are fortunate enough to have received jewelry as a gift from a boyfriend, remember that it is a gift, and need not be returned. It belongs to you. While you may be eager to wash that man right out of your hair, wash your hair but keep the ring or whatever. It is yours to enjoy, and if you can't, put it away for awhile, give it away or sell it later, but you certainly aren't obligated to give it back. If you are actually engaged or married, you should always wear your ring with everything. I only take my wedding rings off to shower or swim. As a matter of fact, chlorine is hard on jewelry, so remove it all before you swim.

Family heirlooms should be kept in the family. If you are fortunate to inherit a piece of family history, guard it closely and cherish it. Even if it is not your taste and you know you will never wear it, plan to pass keep it for your own children or relative and relay the story that undoubtedly goes along with it. Sadly, I lost my grandmother's pearl earrings down the bathroom sink. I was cleaning them in a jewelry cleaner jar, and when I took them out to rinse them they fell out of my hand and went swoosh down the drain. Devastating. Lesson learned, use the sink stopper, but do clean your jewelry regularly.

Shoes

Nothing makes a girl happier faster than a fantastic new pair of shoes. Shoes feel good, and nothing makes you feel sexier than a fresh pedicure and gorgeous shoes. Throw in toe cleavage, too.

Heels

Heels are simply it. But not just any heel, they must be a high, four-inch heel for all-out sex appeal. However, for walking or working, two-and-a-half to three-inch works well. A lower, kitten heel with pants is fine, and I love flats with pants.

Boots

Boots are a wonderful thing. They can be extremely comfortable and keep you warmer and dryer. To create a longer leg line with any length boot, wear an opaque hose in the same color as the boot with a skirt or dress, or a pant in the same color as the boot. I like the look of a skinny pant or legging tucked into the boot. This look comes and goes, and can date you faster than a – never mind. The trick for a lean line is to start with a narrow leg. Put the pant or legging on first, then put a pair of socks on over them and smooth the fabric. Then put on the boot, making sure the sock doesn't show. Preferably the socks, boots and pants are the same color to maximize your leg line.

Sandals

Sandals should only be worn bare-legged. Promise me you will never wear hose with sandals ... ever. Some styles of sandals will enhance the look of your foot, so choose something that will not focus on your flaws, but rather accentuate the positive. Try on lots of pairs to find the best look, perhaps a peep toe! Again, a little heel height is always the most flattering, but flat sandals can work too, just pay attention to how it makes your leg look. When wearing sandals, they should not be too small so that your foot hangs over the back of the shoe, nor should they be too large that there is more than 1/8 inch of the back of the sandal exposed. The small toe should not protrude between the straps.

Wedges

Wedges when in style are fantastic for someone short or with short legs. They give you the comfort of a flatter shoe but the height of a heel. When they aren't in style, please don't wear them. It will date you faster than blue eye shadow.

Patent Leather

Shoes made of patent leather have a bit of a dressier connotation, can easily go from the office to cocktails and are now worn all year around. Did you know a little Vaseline rubbed on the surface of patent leather shines them up quickly? Patent leather does not breathe, so if you plan to do a lot of walking, choose something else instead. Another thing to be cautious of when wearing patent leather shoes is that they can stick together. I know this sounds really weird, but I have a most fabulous pair of Manolo patent leather stiletto pumps. Besides walking on top of skyscrapers, they "catch" each other and can actually force my knees to buckle and take me down. Oh yeah, dangerous. This could be where the term "fashion victim" came from. I prefer, "Fashion Vixen."

Suede
Never use your hands on suede. The natural oils rub off and can discolor the suede. I recommend a suede brush occasionally and suede eraser to remove scuffmarks. These can be found at your shoe repair store. And try not to wear your suede shoes in the rain or snow. They'll be destined for ruin. Suede is just that much more fragile than other materials.

Skins
Shoes made of animal skins are a big investment, but you get a lot of mileage for the price. A pair of good quality crocodile or lizard shoes will last a lifetime if taken good care of. Again, I hearken back to quality not quantity. Stick to a more classic silhouette, a pump or loafer. If you really can't spring for the luxury skins, other skins work well too – ostrich, python or shagreen and many others. Otherwise purchase as good of quality of leather shoe as you can afford. Some of the stamped leathers look as good as the real thing, so educate yourself to what they should look like.

I would rather have a limited number of shoes that work for me, that I can just go to my closet and put on that are comfortable, then have 50 that don't work for various reasons. In case you were wondering, this is what I can't live without:

- Manolo Blahnik black crocodile or lizard pumps (4-inch heel)
- Chanel ballet flats
- Jimmy Choo high, black boots
- strappy sandals in metallic silver or gold
- white, flat sandals
- Converse sneakers

Now, you probably also need sports shoes, and specific-occasion shoes like a pair of Wellies for the outdoors, tennis shoes, riding boots, flip flops for the beach, that kind of thing. In general, shoes should be well maintained. Match the shoe to the occasion. This is where I would like to stress, just shoot yourself if you ever under any circumstance are inclined to wear tennis shoes with a skirt while walking to work. There should be a special place in Jersey where they send people who do this.

OOOOOOUUUUUUUCH. That KILLS me. This is so unattractive and the epitome of schlumpy. Pay attention to what makes your feet and legs look good and what you feel good in. There are plenty of cute flats out there that will make a comfortable choice. You can't be pretty when your feet hurt, and you certainly can't be pretty when you feel just plain oogly.

I must admit, I really don't understand some shoe trends. Ugly shoes are just that – ugly. Shoes should beg to be bought, like jewels catching your eye, in other words, you covet them. It feels sinfully delicious. Now that is a fantastic pair of shoes. Don't be sensible in this category. Sometimes I buy the shoe first, then try to figure out what goes with it, or will purchase something to go with the shoe. Sometimes I start with the shoe when I am getting dressed. I select a beautiful shoe then create an outfit to compliment it. Just say NO to ugly shoes. Forget sensible. Beauty first. What won't work is cheap shoes, or shoes with a chunky heel – face it babe, chunky anything just doesn't cut it. So what if you have to take an ibuprofen to enable you to wear a beautiful pair of Jimmy Choos or Manolo Blahniks. It is worth it – you will feel so much sexier, and the world will see a prettier you with an elongated leg line ... you will look taller, slimmer and infinitely more fashionable.

What is with clicking heels? My gawd, if you care enough to put on heels, spend $5 and have the heel taps replaced at a shoe repair shop. They are all over the place, so you have no excuse. This is one of the tackiest things ever. Nothing like drawing attention to yourself, tap dancing down the street! Since I live in a rainy climate, I put very thin zip soles on the bottom of my shoes (except the divinely red-soled Loboutins or evening shoes) so I won't slip. It is difficult enough to wear heels without the fear of falling. If the toes are very thin, put toe taps on. None of these things are visible, and they will increase the longevity of your investment. Have your shoes polished if necessary, too. It isn't difficult to do this yourself, and is a good part of your clothing maintenance routine.

I knew someone (not me) who, rather than ruining her brand new TDF (To Die For) Manolos in a NYC thunderstorm (cab-less), took them off and walked barefoot all 36 grungy blocks home. What we do for shoes.

Here is a great secret if the balls of your feet tire. At the drugstore, you will find an array of foot products. Buy the foam cushioned shoe liners, lift up the lining of the shoe (easiest to get a grip at the heel or the instep) and pull. It should lift right up and or out. Then put the foam liner down, and replace the shoe liner. If it doesn't stick well enough, I just use some glue stick or glue. The foam liner creates an instant cushion. This is particularly helpful if you are on your feet all day or night. And you can't be pretty if your feet hurt. If they do, soak them in Epsom salts, massage with essential oils, have a pedicure. Shoes should fit well. Quite simply, the shoe provides the exclamation point at the end of our ensemble!

Hose

If you have good legs, use a self tanner for a hint of color. (We never tan, because of obvious risk of skin cancer, premature aging, and all that.) Nothing is sexier than a beautiful leg in a beautiful shoe with a glimpse of a beautiful pedicure. HOWEVER, if you have fat calves, short stubby legs, live for the winter. Dark opaque hose hide a multitude of sins. Again, think of elongating (I don't know anyone too tall and thin!) so a monochromatic leg line is the best.

Cinnamon or suntan hose is a forever a never – if you must wear a nude hose for work or something, find a color that closely matches your skin tone and is sheer. The technology has improved so much, there is myriad of choices available. Your hose should not have reinforced heels and toes, are you kidding me? I still see women wearing reinforcement with open, peep-toed shoes or sandals. Can you even imagine a more disdainful sight? UGH.

Patterned hose is fun for the fall and winter. Keep in mind the total look and don't over pattern yourself. Fishnets are sexy, and I like them best with something simple so the attention is on your legs and they don't compete with everything else. Probably not appropriate for work unless you are in fashion and it is a big fishnet season.

Belts

Many styles and widths are available. Sometimes belts are in, and sometimes they are out, sometimes they are wide, sometimes they are narrow. Sometimes they are worn high to create an empire effect, sometimes they are worn low and slouch across the hips, or sometimes worn at the waist. Belts can emphasize the waist or the hips. They can add definition and interest to an outfit. If worn incorrectly, a belt can be a disaster. Never buckle or tie a belt too tight – hence, the muffin top effect. Remember that a belt is an accessory, just as a scarf, or jewelry. When in doubt, take one thing off.

Let a great belt be the focal point, and tone down or eliminate other accessories. Knowing your body and developing an eye is critical to making it all work as one cohesive statement. To belt or not to belt, that is the question.

Gloves

A necessity in certain climates, gloves protect your hands from the elements. The perfect dress glove is cashmere-lined kidskin leather. The ¾-length hits above the wrist and keeps you warmer. Buy the same style so if you lose one chances are you'll have an extra replacement. I spent the first half of my life constantly losing my gloves. I never go anywhere in cooler weather without them. Remember Michelle Obama's contrasting green gloves that were the fashion statement of the Inaugural? They didn't compete with other accessories. The green gloves were "it," and what a statement they made.

Sunglasses

These can make you look mysterious, help the health of your eyes, and block the sun from damaging the skin around your eyes. It also lets you look at people without them knowing it. You've got to love that. They are a must, not just an accessory. Besides, sunglasses convey tons of attitude.

Try on lots, again, to find the right look. Don't be afraid, sunglasses can say more about you than anything else. Avoid the same shape as your face shape, in other words, if you have a round face, steer clear of round sunglasses. If you are light skinned with blue eyes, choose a dark shade. Once I bought a fantastic pair of Dior sunglasses with light blue shades, and I could only wear them inside. It is nice if you can develop a wardrobe of sunglasses with various degrees of shading and styling. Keep them free of fingerprints, and store them in their original case to prevent scratches and breakage. If you lose a pin or they become stretched (this occurs if you often wear them up on your head like a headband) then take them to an optometrist shop and they usually repair them for you for a minimal or no charge. If you wear prescription glasses, consider contact lenses or laser surgery. You can often purchase high quality fashion frames and just change the lenses. There is no need to settle for dowdy outdated frames. A fabulous pair of sunglasses could quite simply be the only accessory you ever need.

Scarves

Scarves are an instant lift. Choose one in silk or cotton, in a large x square as it is the most versatile. My personal favorites are from Hermés. Scarves go in cyclical trends also, but I always favor the Audrey Hepburn look of a head wrap, or tied casually around the neck. They can look too contrived if meant to stay in place and look perfect. You'll drive yourself crazy, too. It takes confidence and certain panache to carry off a silk scarf. Imagine yourself on the Côte d'Azur in a fabulous sports car. Channel Princess Grace. Besides, you'll have an automatic "triangle" tie and voilà, a new top! I keep mine pressed, folded and stacked in the drawer. The easiest way to wear a scarf is to fold opposite ends together to make a triangle, throw it over your shoulders and tie loosely in front. Très Parisienne.

A small "twilly" scarf adds color and personality tied around a handbag strap or around your neck, ponytail or wrist in a small knot. Oblong scarves also look great worn these ways or just hanging down long around the neck. Oblong is the best shape for wrapping around your waist as a sash, or for tying into a bow. Larger cotton scarves work well as a pareo at the beach or pool. Learn to tie them around your waist as a skirt. For a dress cover-up, just fold in a triangle and take the two ends and pull up around your neck and tie at the back of your neck. Another way to wear them is folded into a triangle and throw over one shoulder, so the middle is on the top of your shoulder and one end hangs down the front and the other end down the back. Pashminas and shawls work well as an evening wrap, as an extra layer in cold weather, or as a summer wrap when the evening cools. These are so versatile, and a great pop of color, too.

Hats

Baseball caps have their purpose; in sports cars, boating, on the tennis court, jogging. Wear them where they are appropriate, in a casual, athletic environment. Hats take guts to wear. Put on the hat and pile on the attitude. Hats with brims should be worn low on the forehead, so you literally need to look up a little to see where you are going. Practice kissing someone, especially if wearing a big hat. Men love hats. there is something very mysterious about them and they fantasize about taking them off and unveiling a beautiful you underneath – sound familiar? Like jeans, it is best to try on several to help you make the best selection. Church or luncheon hats should be kept in their original hatbox. Replace the stay inside the rim and stuff with tissue to retain its shape. If someone happens to sit on your favorite hat, it may be repairable.

Trunk Shows

Does the opportunity to meet a fashion expert and get their advice on what looks good on you personally sound appealing? Are you too busy to spend much time shopping? Do you want to be guaranteed to get first pick? Then trunk shows could be a good thing for you.

Trunk shows are when the designer or their representative brings the next season's collection to the store for a preview. This is commonly done on higher end merchandise that is cut to order. So, the fall trunk shows occur in late spring, and the spring trunk shows occur in late Fall or a season ahead. This gives the customer an opportunity to see the collection in its entirety, rather than just what that store's buyer has selected for the store. You also have the advantage of being the first to see the new trends of the upcoming season. For me, the best advantage is that the designer or their representative is at the store in person with the collection to help you. They are a wealth of information about the collection's specifics. They can tell you everything you want to know about the fabrics, the care of the garment, how the designer accessorized it on the runway, what would look best on you, what to wear it with. They provide a different point of view than your salesperson. Since they represent this one collection only, they know it inside and out. Your salesperson, on the other hand, has a more general understanding of the store's offerings and a broader, big-picture expertise.

I was flying on my company's jet across country to an event early on in Stella McCartney's career when she designed for Chloé. We arrived late, as we had to switch to a commercial jet due to minor mechanical difficulties. We ended up being forced to change into cocktail attire in the airport bathroom. Not an easy trick. My boss, who was always beautifully put together, quickly slipped into her new Chloé blouse and skirt. It wasn't until the photo in WWD appeared the following week that I realized she had the blouse on backwards! Sometimes you have to pay attention to the way things are supposed to be worn, as it is not always logical. This is when the expertise of the sales representative who could have explained how it was to be worn, would have paid off.

During a trunk show, you have the opportunity to order pieces that may not be carried in the store, or "reserve" pieces off the "on order" of the store. They bring their collection in sample size only, so unless you are the same size as their fit model or runway models, you can only look at what you are buying. This takes some education. Hopefully, the store will have current season stock in at the same time so you can determine what size works best from this particular designer. (See next chapter, SIZE MATTERS)

If you see something that is perfect and a "must have," you will then place an order. Be sure you know how much it is, when it is expected to be delivered, which is just an approximation, and what recourse you have if it doesn't work out. Depending on the store, they may require a deposit that could be non-refundable, or they could require you to pay a portion or up to 100% of the price. You should not be charged shipping, and if you are, negotiate this. You may incur alteration costs if you need any alterations done, unless this is made-to-measure. This often confuses people, but these designers have standard sizes and if you need the pants shortened or the sleeves lengthened that would need to be done by the store's fitter.

The salesperson will take all of your information, and you need to make sure you have a receipt with all pertinent information, including cost, deposit amount if anything, specifically what you have ordered including size and color, as well as the estimated delivery date. You should ask if when it arrives it isn't what you expected or you have changed your mind, are you still obligated to take it, and if not, is your deposit 100% refundable?

Then, once the designer has shipped your merchandise and it arrives in the store, you will be notified.

Unless it is clearly stated that this is a non-refundable purchase, keep the tags on and keep track of the receipt. Sometimes things do look differently once we get them home. The color doesn't match what I intended it to go with, I look fatter in it than in the store's mirror, or I have something just like it. Sound familiar? Sometimes it takes me several days to decide, but once you do, return or exchange it right away. It is irresponsible not to return his or her inventory in season so the store has an opportunity to sell it to someone else at full price. Be honest with the salesperson too. It is all about trust and rapport, so explain why it didn't work and what might be a better choice for you now or in the future. This gives the salesperson a reason to call you and will help maintain the relationship. Don't be embarrassed, everyone makes mistakes. You can always hold something, too, though, if you are really unsure. There are times when this might be the best option.

Size Matters (or does it?)

We are all too hung up on size. It is just a number. Every manufacturer uses a different fit model. There is no consistency on sizing across the world, so you can be a size 4 in an American designer like Donna Karan, a size 8 in a junior designer, and a size 2 at J Crew. Forget the Europeans! It can be really frustrating because you are a different size in a particular garment than you thought you were. If I don't know the store or the brands, I try on several sizes in the same thing. We get caught up in the notion that we are a "6" or now down to a size "10." This means nothing! Whatever you do, don't buy a size if it doesn't fit. We rarely lose the weight we hope to, and if that is the case, you'll have a closet full of clothes you can't wear. Even more importantly, don't berate yourself if you are a size or two larger in something than you thought. It is completely irrelevant, and doesn't necessarily mean you have gained or lost weight.

European sizing tends to run narrower in the hip, shoulders and bust. American sizing for women runs fuller in the hip, shoulders and bust. A junior fit is shorter in the rise, narrower in the hips and bust, A contemporary fit is somewhere in between. Within these categories, there is also a large variance in the specifications. So try it on, and if you really must, cut out the size tag before you wear it.

Women's approximate size conversion chart

Italian	36	38	40	42	44	46	48	50
French	34	36	38	40	42	44	46	48
American	0	2	4	6	8	10	12	14

Retail Therapy

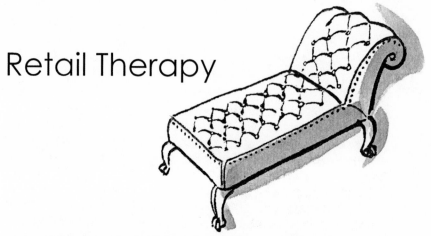

Men do not understand retail therapy. I really think you need to have a mature conversation about this at the onset of a relationship. This is one of the most argued-about subjects in a relationship. My husband nearly died when the subject came up about my face cream being $350.00 a jar. But I haven't had plastic surgery, and I am not currently seeing a therapist, so he figures he is getting off easy. Negotiate. Besides, the cream is going to keep my skin young and beautiful, right? Men are very logical and visual on every level – if you didn't already know that, you mustn't ever forget it! More importantly, I tell him how much I saved. So if I spent $1,000.00 but the regular price was $1,500.00 I approach it as I just saved $500.00 and look what I got! It sounds so simplistic, and it is.

If nothing else, it should prompt a good laugh. I love a bargain, because it means you can have more. So if I buy a piece on sale, then I show him the sales tag/receipt so he can see how much I have saved. I also keep him apprised of my store reward points or dividends. He loves that. So figure out what ways he will feel the benefit. (Besides you looking incredible and feeling fabulous). You need a career for several reasons, but you definitely need it for bargaining power.

Now I am the first to have "The Urge to Splurge." Sometimes it is just plain fun to shake it up a bit. "When I grow old I want to wear purple" – don't wait, do it now! Developing your personal sense of style doesn't mean you can't do something different. We all have moods or phases and it's fun to experiment, too. Deviate, and when you feel the urge to splurge occasionally and as your budget allows, do it! Buy a frivolous piece once in a while and don't feel guilty. Don't spend a ton on it, though, or you won't have enough $$ for the quality investment pieces. Consider yourself forewarned, you may require therapy if retail therapy becomes excessive. If you can't pay cash for things, no matter how terrific the bargain is, then please stop. If you buy more than you can possibly fit in your closet, stop. If you feel high when you buy, and low when you go, stop. If you find yourself making excuses or hiding packages in the refrigerator or under the hood of your car, stop. If you feel excessive remorse or guilt, call your therapist (preferably a woman who will help you with perspective). On the other hand, if you don't feel any of these things, go for it sister!

Girl On The Go

Traveling has become challenging, but if you keep current on the TSA requirements, and do your homework, especially when traveling abroad, you can make it easier. Here are some of the things I've learned that might help you. I lay out my clothes a few days ahead of time so I can see what I might be missing. I actually pack the night before, not too much more ahead of time than that though, otherwise you'll increase the wrinkle factor. Don't wait until the last minute to pack either. There are too many details involved to do it all at the last minute, so that's way too stressful. Inevitably, you will forget something, or pack things that don't get worn, because they don't go with anything else you brought. Just be organized, and plan for the unexpected. I Google a new hotel to get as much information about it as possible. You can always call the concierge and ask them what you need to know, too. If you don't regularly maintain your wardrobe, such as mending, picking up your dry cleaning, having your shoes repaired, then I suggest you make two lists the week before leaving on a trip. Make a list of what you want to pack. Make another list of what on the first list you must repair or get in order first. Prioritize it so you have everything done and ready to go two days before you leave. This will actually save you time in the long run, keeping you from last minute running around.

On a summer flight from JFK to Mumbai via Paris, the 'au naturel' odor was too pungent to imagine. I literally could not breathe. This prompted me to always wear a turtleneck or a scarf when I fly. Spray a mist of perfume on your neck, or lightly on the neckline of the sweater so you can inhale it if something stinky wafts past you. I am always cold on a flight, so I'll carry a pashmina shawl in the summer and a cashmere shawl in the winter to use as a blanket. Layering is essential. I also take a pair of jelly flip-flops in the summer or a disposable pair of anklets to put on to go through TSA so I don't have to go barefoot. I carry a small cosmetic bag with the necessary cosmetics just in case my checked luggage doesn't make it. Include a lip balm, a nasal spray and hand lotion. You might also carry a change of clothes so you have something to change in to if your luggage is lost. Generally, though, I have had so many experiences where my luggage was lost for days, or had things stolen out of my bag that I rarely check my baggage. I recommend checking the TSA website before you start packing to see what new changes there are to the security check in process.

Check the weather forecast for the duration of your stay. Not that the weather can't change, as we know, but it will keep you from bringing a raincoat and boots or other things you won't need to wear if it is going to be sunny the entire time.

Buy a bottle of flat non-sparkling water before you board the plane (carbonated water causes bloating), and healthy snacks (yogurt, nuts, a banana) – you never know how long you will be on a flight. You can be sitting on the runway, the plane can be diverted, any number of things can happen. Be prepared and you will be more comfortable and less stressed out. Go to the ladies room before you board, too. Sometimes you can sit on the runway before takeoff as it can be a long time before the "fasten seat belt" sign goes off.

The other essentials to pack for winter travel are a foldable umbrella, warm hat, and tights. I also travel with either a nylon Prada tote or a larger Longchamps tote that take up virtually no room in my luggage, but can become another piece of luggage if I need them. This is essential for big city shopping trips, or for traveling with children as you always come home with more than you left with.

Most hotels will provide a bathrobe and slippers. If they aren't already in the room when you arrive, call housekeeping and ask for them. The same goes for an alarm clock, hair dryer, sewing kit, emery board, soap, toothbrush and toothpaste if you forgot them. You can always borrow a big umbrella from the hotel if you prefer.

Travel jewelry is a great thing. Leave your good pieces in the safety deposit box or better yet at home. Buy big, bold fun costume jewelry for travel. You won't be devastated if you forget it on the nightstand at the hotel. If you must travel with your good jewelry, take only what you can wear, and tone it down to a non Las Vegas bling level. Don't check expensive luggage or any luggage with a club id tag. And whatever you do, don't pack expensive items in your checked luggage.

My luggage was broken in to at JFK on my way to Paris one time. Besides a camera, I'd packed several of my favorite pieces, including three Chanel handbags, my Dior makeup case, and a new cashmere cardigan that was going to be an essential piece that trip to wear over everything. They took that because I hadn't removed the sales tags yet, so they probably thought they could return it for cash. They didn't steal any other clothes, thank goodness. That is one way to look at your cup as half full, and lesson learned. Consequently, my advice is to always carry on your luggage, and try not to ever check it. If you must, you can usually gate check it if the overhead bins are too full. That way, you get to pick up the bag the minute you step off the plane without it going to baggage claim.

I pride myself on being a fantastic packer. I've had to do it for years for business, and love to travel for pleasure as well. The single most important rule is not to pack more than you yourself can handle. The second most important rule is to decide on a color scheme and stick with it. Your outfits will be more interchangeable and you will bring less with you because everything works with everything else. This allows you more room to bring home those souvenirs as well.

It's best to use several small cosmetic bags rather than one large one. It is much harder to find the room for the large one, and it is usually the last thing you pack before you leave for the airport. With several small soft bags you can fit them in the small spots more easily in your luggage. Also, I keep them organized, so in one I have my eyelash curler, tweezers, and small magnifying mirror. Another bag has vitamins and any disaster control things that I don't use every day, like Band-aids. Another one has non-liquid makeup that doesn't have to go through the quart bag in airport security. That would be makeup brushes, powdered eye shadow, face powder, lipstick that I don't carry in my handbag. Then I pack separately what I can't live without (in case your luggage gets lost) every small size sample and product imaginable in the quart size bag. Ask for fragrance samples, and anything else you need when you are purchasing the full size cosmetic. Also, larger drug stores have a section for travel-sized products like toothpaste and deodorant, which is helpful. Keep any prescriptions with you in your handbag. Some other things I can't live without include antiseptic wipes (I wipe down the armrests and trays when I get seated on the plane), Visine, and nasal spray to keep my nasal passages hydrated and less susceptible to colds and infections. A little neurotic, for sure.

Layer & Folding Techniques

First, place shoes on the bottom of the suitcase, heel to toe opposite of each other. Stuff the shoes with hose, socks, or something else small that won't stretch the shoes, but will help them maintain their shape. Then place them in fabric shoe bags to keep everything in place and any dirt from the bottom of your shoes away from everything else. The bottom layer of the suitcase should be level, so you might need to put something else there to make it flat. Next, fold a pair of pants in half lengthwise, as if you are looking at them from the side angle (crease to crease). Place them on top of the shoe layer, so that the middle section rests in the suitcase and the top and bottom hang over each end of the suitcase. Then add additional pants in the same manner. Next, fold one end in of the whole pile of pants, and then the other end of the whole pile. Smooth out any wrinkles as you fold. Lie out each sweater and place a piece of white (non-acidic) tissue paper flat on the knit and fold in sleeves then fold in half lengthwise. Pile these and place on one end of the suitcase. Each of these layers should be flat and the full length of the suitcase.

Keep jackets and dresses individually on the hangers, with a plastic dry cleaner bag over each item, using the hanging fold out portion of the luggage. Layer any shirts or blouses under the jackets to maximize the space.

When you reach your destination, you can lay the tissue down for protection in the shelves as you unpack. And do unpack immediately upon reaching your destination. Hang up as much as possible to let the wrinkles hang out. Do this before you make a phone call or go out. It is a very good habit to acquire, and can save you time ironing or sending things out to be pressed. It really does make a huge difference if you travel with knits and pieces that don't have a natural wrinkle tendency. One way to tell the wrinkle factor is by the hand test. Place a small corner of the fabric in one hand and make a fist for a couple of seconds. Undo your fist, and shake the fabric a few times. A minimal amount or no wrinkling at all means it is a winner. If it stays wrinkled looking, pass. If you wear shirts, use a shirt folder – it works really well. You fold the shirt to the guide size that comes with it, enabling you to pack more efficiently.

Avoid loose things in your luggage. Too many times I've seen people's luggage open on the carousel and things falling out and getting damaged. If you do check luggage, check the weight restrictions for the airline. We tend to pack more if we are checking our luggage, and now with new weight restrictions you may end up paying to take that extra outfit.

Wear something a bit more businesslike on the plane. Comfort is key, but avoid looking like a bag lady or someone who is going jogging. Believe it or not, you might get treated better or possibly upgraded if you look good. Besides, I've heard they save the well-dressed people first. It's worth a try. I also try to wear the bulkier things, like the coat, sweater and perhaps boots that would otherwise take up an inordinate amount of room in the suitcase.

Here are some examples of what to pack for a 3-day business trip to a city, a 5-day winter vacation, and a 2-week vacation at a beach resort:

3-day Business Trip

- Dark colored pantsuit (black or navy)
- Skirt that can work back to jacket of pantsuit
- A knit underpinning to pair back to the cardigan as a tee
- Twin set to wear with the dark pants of the pantsuit on the plane and/or for a casual dinner
- Chemise or shirtdress that can go to a business dinner or be worn for day if the weather is warm, with the cardigan (depending on your type of business, and what is considered acceptable)
- Raincoat (I love the nylon ones that fold up to nothing)
- Umbrella (small and foldable)
- Pashmina
- Night gown
- Lingerie
- Workout clothes
- Essentials – straightening iron; that sort of thing
- Flats
- Pumps or dress boots
- Flip-flops

Wear one of the jackets with a pair of the pants (matching or not) if you are headed straight into the office. Otherwise, wear the twin set with the pants. Pack the raincoat (scrunched up into gallon-sized Zip lock bag) in the tote bag.

if you expect rain at your destination. Wear shoes that slip off easily, and bring along rubber unadorned flip flops or socks to avoid going barefoot through security screening and for walking around the hotel room.

Carry on a small wheelie bag, put your work/laptop in a tote with a small handbag inside. Collect nice lingerie bags and assorted small zipper bags to keep your things organized. You will be especially appreciative if the TSA starts looking through your things. Also, bring along a few extra zip lock bags. I always pack a few large ones in case I need them for an ice bag or to pack something wet on the way home. They also work as a dirty clothes bag. Put the dirty socks or flip-flops in a Ziploc bag after clearing security and before adding to your suitcase. You want everything to stay clean in your luggage.

Once you are through security screening, take a large bottle of water, and drink it to stay hydrated. Not only do you feel better when you arrive, your skin looks better too.

Take something good to read or a work project as it helps pass the time. You never know when you will be delayed, often for hours. This will also help you avoid the gabby lonely person seated next to you. Lastly, include a shawl to keep you warm and cozy. Don't use the airline blanket (scratchy and germy) if you can help it, and then, only if it is freshly wrapped in plastic. Cooties.

5-day Winter Vacation

- Jeans
- Turtleneck sweater (wear on the plane)
- Cute snow boots if snow is predicted (wear on the plane)
- two pairs of pants

- Two twin sets, so you can wear the underpinning under a jacket and layer the cardigan over your shoulders.
- Coat (wool or cashmere, and layer the shawl for warmth)
- Black cashmere shawl
- Cocktail Dress (jersey or lightweight knit)
- Boots or pumps that can go from day to evening.
- Walking shoes – ballet flats, loafers, boots, whatever you prefer
- Knit dress or basic black dress for dinner
- Thin layer of silk long underwear
- Lingerie
- Tights
- Workout and sports-specific clothes
- Cosmetics/Essentials
- Gloves, warm hat, extra socks and silk long underwear for an extra non-bulky layer if needed.

Be prepared. Winter weather can be tricky, so check the 10-day forecast, and be prepared for anything. Winter travel is much more bulky and cumbersome and takes more luggage space. Really think of layering and plan to wear everything more than once. You can launder your tights, lingerie and knitwear yourself, if you have to.

2-week Beach Vacation

- Fabulous swimwear – two to three bikinis or maillots
- Pareos, tunics and beach cover-ups (at least two)
- White jeans

- Shorts or short skirt
- four tops or t-shirts
- Two sundresses for lunches, shopping, dinner. Look for silk jersey (so packable) and cotton knit (so breathable).
- Cardigan
- Pashmina
- Sun hat with a big brim/baseball cap for active wear
- Sunglasses
- Flip-flops
- Mid-high-heeled sandals for shopping, dinner and going out
- Tennis or golf clothes or other sports-specific items
- Night gown or cami and boy/shorts
- Beach jewelry

A great body is your best accessory. Add a bikini, some flip-flops, sunscreen, sunglasses and you are good to go. The best thing about summer beach travel is that it is so minimal.

I'm never without a scented candle, to remind me of home and to eliminate any hotel odor. The Donna Karan mist candles are tiny and have a very mild scent that helps to neutralize odor. I also take my own pillowcase. When I worked in the south of France, the hotel literally soaked the linens in bleach, and consequently I woke up the first morning there to swollen eyes and red splotches all over my face. I have a friend who insists on traveling with her own lightweight silk sheets that fold up to nothing. Not a bad idea if you have sensitive skin.

Laundering

Anything containing wool or silk, send to the dry cleaners. However, I learned many years ago while working in the Couture showrooms in Paris that the preferred method of cleaning fine garments is simply airing them out, literally hanging them on a hanger in front of an open window. Fresh air is the best air freshener. How's that for a play on words. The cleaning fluids are not only bad for the environment, but wreak havoc with fibers. This makes sense, right? They make the garment smell like chemicals too. Green cleaners are sprouting up everywhere, so that is a better alternative. But spot clean washables if you can. I also wash a lot of things on delicate, in cold water with Dreft or by hand in Woolite and line dry or lie flat to dry. It takes more work, granted, but saves money and improves the longevity of the garment, besides the environment. Do not, however, try to pre treat stains when you intend to dry clean the garment. It will just make matters worse. Best to tell the cleaners what the spot is if you know, and get it to them as quickly as possible before the stain settles in for good.

I do think it wise to follow the fabric care labels on garments for optimum care. If the label has a big red X and says don't do it, don't. Be mindful that they are covering themselves from liability by doing this and often there is a better method than the one they recommend if you are careful and become experienced at laundering.

If pilling occurs use a cashmere comb. I always wash my own cashmere sweaters, I never dry clean them.

I've made the mistake by investing in too many expensive white pieces. The dry cleaning fluids cause whites to gray eventually. Now unless it is cotton or linen, or a less-expensive item that I'm not investing in, I won't purchase white. If you do take white garments to the dry cleaner, ask them to use fresh solvents, as they will often reuse the same for many garments. They have never charged me any more to do this, so just ask.

Dry clean all pieces of a set at the same time. In other words, take the pant and jacket of a suit both in at the same time to ensure they will continue to match. Remove the plastic bags from clothing as soon as you get it home. Natural fibers need to breathe.

Missing buttons should be replaced; hems kept neatly, holes darned, basic maintenance. I usually keep a shopping bag in my closet of things that need repair and do it all at one time. I keep another bag for pieces that need dry cleaning. Simplify and keep yourself organized.

Save the extra buttons, thread or beads attached to any garments you purchase. Keep them all in a box so you have them if you get a moth hole in something; lose a button, or whatever. Sometimes you can do the repairs easily yourself, but if not, your dry cleaner or alterations person should be able to make the repair for you.

Hats can be re-shaped, belts shortened or lengthened at a shoe repair shop, and many things can be remade into something else entirely. So don't give up on something that you love that just needs a little sprucing.

A list for your Closet Toolbox:

- lint brush
- masking tape
- de-piller
- suede brush
- assorted needles and thread
- sewing shears
- small and large safety pins
- hairspray or static cling spray
- nail glue
- antiseptic wipes
- shoe polish
- extra buttons
- jewelry cleaner

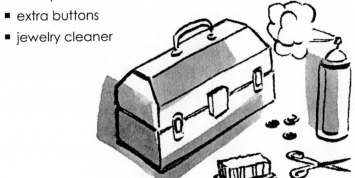

In The Closet

Organizing closets is one of my favorite pastimes. I can't believe I am actually admitting that but there you go. It brings me immense gratification. You begin with a mess, organize it, and end with something beautiful and extremely functional.

Many people say they never have enough room in their closet so they can't begin to organize it. Well, that's ridiculous. The first step just requires you to take everything out of the closet and throw it on the bed. Then clean the closet of the years of dust that has accumulated. Now make piles:

- one pile to throw away, pieces that are torn, or otherwise unusable

- one pile to resale or to swap with friends, good pieces that you just won't ever wear again

- one pile to charity, pieces that are too good to throw away, and unable to be resold

- one pile for summer clothes (only very light clothes that you wear only in the summer)

- one pile for winter clothes (only very heavy clothes that you only wear in winter)

You will have a transitional pile that will stay in your closet all year long. This includes anything medium weight like gabardine, medium weight cashmere sweaters, cotton shirts and silk blouses, that kind of thing. If you don't do that, you will find you need to go searching in the tote boxes or backup closet and that is time consuming and frustrating.

Once you have done this, put everything back in your closet depending on the season. So let's assume it is fall. Begin categorizing by classification. I start with pants. Put all the pants together by color. Like on a color wheel, light to dark. So on one end is winter white, then beige, camels, browns, navy, gray and black. I would say my closet is at least 1/2 black, so within the blacks I organize it even further. I do it by fabric, but you could organize them however best works for you, such as casual and dressy.

Next you would organize your skirts in the same way. When I get to brown or black again, I own a lot so I group them together by pleated, straight, long, short, prints, and patterns.

I separate my suits into the jacket, skirt and pant categories. This way, I have more options, and it helps me be more creative about how I put myself together. Sometimes I love the jacket of a suit but may not have the same feeling about the pants for one reason or another. Perhaps the fit isn't quite right (then they should go in the "to be altered" pile) or the jacket still looks really great but the skirt is a little dated. This happens. Continue with jackets. I like to keep mine first by color again, then within the blacks for instance, I keep them by length. It might seem strange, but it is just the way I think, so it is easy for me. The short jackets, waist-length, hip-length, ¾-length and long jackets are all separated.

Blouses and shirts just need colorizing. I have mostly white shirts so it is pretty straightforward for me, but if you have a lot in this classification, colorizing is the simplest way to organize them. Dresses would be last. I keep these by sleeve length rather than color. I put all the sundresses together, chemises together (OK, then by color) short-sleeve and then long-sleeve dresses together. As in every category, you can organize it by what you own, these are just examples. Basically, organize by color, shape, and fabric, whatever the dominant themes are within each classification.

Knitwear is best kept folded. The reason for this is that knits can lose their shape and stretch. Ideally, you would fold them with tissue. Lay the sweater on a flat surface, place a piece of white acid free tissue on it, fold one third of one side in, then the next side so they touch but do not overlap, and are over the tissue. Then fold one sleeve in over the side with the shoulder making a 45° angle. If there is a turtleneck, lay it back at the neckline. Then fold back in half. Voilà! This does take a lot of practice. If you want immediate assistance, go to a fabulous boutique or specialty store and watch them do it. Keep knits colorized and within the color keep them categorized. So, for example, within the blacks, you'll have evening together, cardigans, turtlenecks, skimpy tops (tanks and halters) and miscellaneous.

I keep my jeans folded. I always have a few favorite pairs that just end up on top of the pile. If you have enough hanging space in your closet or dressing area, or a lot of jeans, then hanging them on hangers is fine.

For lingerie, I keep my tights and hose in one drawer, again, using drawer dividers. Then I keep my bras and panties together by color, because now you know I always match. I have one drawer for blacks, one for whites, one for nudes, and one for pretty colors. I have a drawer for sports bras, panties and another for specialty lingerie.

Organize your shoes by category as well, then by color within each category. I like to keep mine in the original boxes, and I locate them by keeping them categorized, and then reading the labels. I have several friends who take a Polaroid of the shoes and staple it onto the front of the box. If you are fortunate enough to have shoe bins or shoe racks built into your closet system, keep them colorized within each classification. Boots need to have boot trees in them to help them retain their shape.

Handbags are an investment, and you never know when you'll want to resurrect one. I keep them by size, so my large tote bags are together, regular schlepper bags, day/workhorse bags, smaller luncheon bags, evening bags, and then my collection of straw bags. They are kept standing up, not piled, so I can access them easily and they don't get crushed. I stuff them with tissue paper so they are full but not overstuffed, and then stored in their original cloth bags if they have one.

Hangers should be consistent, and they don't need to be expensive. Hang all your shirts facing in the same direction, on the same type of hanger. These can be from the dry cleaner, which is desirable if you are limited on space. Hang all your pants on pants hangers. Hang pants front to back not side to side. These will take up less room than folded over a hanger, plus you won't have that lovely crease line from the fold when you go to wear it. If you are short on hanging space, use thin hangers to create more room or tiered hangers. Leave space between the hangers for the air to circulate, hence allowing the clothes to breathe.

Put like colors together, and hang them light to dark as if on a color wheel. Do the same for your shoes and accessories. I keep my accessories by category as well. My collection of silk scarves are all folded and stacked in piles by color. My belts are kept coiled in a drawer divider, however the big fashion belts are kept on hooks in my closet. Gloves are kept stacked in a separate drawer, as are sunglasses and other small accessories.

Storage and closet stores abound, and they carry terrific products and can often customize your closet for you. If you go this route, you should map out what your needs are and take the time to think it through carefully.

I also think it is a wonderful thing to create a dressing area, even if it is only a tiny corner of your bedroom next to your closet. Use scented drawer liners, cedar chips, room spray, a fabulous scented candle, anything that will help keep the moths away and your environment relaxing and smelling wonderful. Hang a full length mirror and somewhere to hang pieces to get an overview of what you are putting together, either for a particular occasion, or when packing for a trip. I recommend trying on an outfit at home prior to actually wearing it. That way, if you are wearing it with shoes or accessories you already have, you will be sure it works. There is nothing worse than having just five minutes left to get ready to go, when you discover some disaster like a rip, a spot, or a wrinkle on something. Try on a complete outfit before the first time you wear it, too, to be sure it is ready to go.

Once you do become organized, it is important to stay organized. You need to go through your closet at least twice a year and EDIT. I do this when I swap out winter for summer and summer for winter. If you haven't worn something in a year get rid of it – unless, of course, it is a fabulous designer piece that you love. In that case, keep anything signature, in perfect condition, or that you wore for a special occasion. These pieces will increase in value both as a vintage piece and for sentimental reasons. I can't tell you the fabulous pieces I've edited too soon. I really could still enjoy that 10-year-old Missoni maxi dress with matching cardigan.

Gorgeous-ness

Hair

I have been coloring my hair since I was 20, and fortunately, it is happier and healthier now than in my teens. Of course, I have a fabulous hairdresser that I adore. If you are going to this expense, (don't try this at home – really scary) be sure to maintain it – every 4-6 weeks approximately, depending on your rate of hair growth. If you are happy with your natural hair color you are lucky, and in the minority. If you are going various shades of gray and/or it is dry and frizzy there is absolutely no reason in this day and age that you need to go there. I consider my hair color a very basic part of my beauty regimen, like brushing my teeth and washing my face.

Get regular trims and keep the style current. Keep your hair trimmed whatever the style is. Neat and tidy and well kept is the mantra. Really long hair is only attractive if it is really healthy, kept regularly trimmed, blunt cut and never below your waist. My favorite longer length is the middle of the back and cut very blunt. Leave the longer lengths to the girls with healthy hair. If yours tends to the frizzy or thin, it will look richer cut in a style. Layering can give the illusion of more body and thickness, but can be more difficult to style.

Keep your hair squeaky clean. If you need to wash your hair every day, please do. Otherwise, if you can stretch it an extra day or more, definitely do. Excessive washing and the heat from blow-drying and flat irons, and chemicals like chlorine really dry out your hair and strip it of natural oils. Figure out a cute hairdo for that day before you wash your hair to help you stretch out the time. Don't neglect the products – use conditioner. One thing I like to do is let my hair dry naturally as often as possible, particularly in the summer.

Don't be afraid to try a new hairstyle every now and then to spice things up. However, when you find something that works for you, stick with it for a while, but not forever. Hairstyles, like fashion do change. An outdated hairstyle will age you as fast as anything. Trust your stylist to recommend the appropriate hair products for you. Have him/her teach you how to blow dry and style your hair. Practice, practice, practice.

Hair accessories are fun to accumulate and come in handy in a pinch. I love tortoiseshell, coral, and anything natural. Some rhinestone clips, barrettes, headbands, ponytail holders, and you are good to go.

Body Hair

Lose it. Laser is the best way to get rid of it. Waxing works too, but is more painful and only temporary. Shaving is the most economical, less painful way. It all needs to go regardless of the method, everywhere, except on your head, eyebrows, and eyelashes. I've even had my face lasered before, too. It really takes the peach fuzz off, gives your face a much smoother look, and your makeup application looks flawless. Do whichever hair removal method you prefer, just do it on a consistent basis.

Laser Hair Removal

This is expensive, but can have long lasting results. There has been great advancement in laser technology so do some investigating or ask friends to refer you to someone. I went to my dermatologist for this treatment and recommend you do so too. This treatment is more expensive than waxing or shaving but the results are impressive. Over the long term, this was a savings to me over waxing. A lot depends on the amount of hair you have, how your hair grows, and how much of your body you want to do.

Start with a small area of your body and see if you like it. I think laser works the best for the bikini area and face if you can afford it. Laser hair removal is relatively painless, as beauty treatments go, but I recommend taking ibuprofen ½ hour before your appointment.

Waxing

Go to a reliable salon for this treatment. Cleanliness is paramount. Waxing is not as long lasting as laser hair removal, but longer lasting than shaving. Schedule your appointment for the week after your period. The pain will be more intense if you wax near ovulation. Exfoliate with a gentle scrub the day before your appointment to remove dead skin that can cause ingrown hairs. I like Clarins body scrub but there are many good ones on the market. Do not exfoliate the day of your appointment because your skin will be slightly irritated. The hair should be at least ¼" long so the wax has something to grip on to. Take an ibuprofen ½ hour before your appointment to minimize the ouch factor. Applying a numbing cream helps, too, and you can buy these over the counter at the drug store. Afterwards, apply a salicylic acid treatment immediately after waxing to calm the area and keep it breakout free. Continue to do this daily if you are prone to irritation.

My virgin voyage to Travis in the Burberry plaid jeans was, well, more than I could ever have anticipated. I decided to do the full-bikini deal, as well as my underarms. But what I expected and what it turned out to be were two completely different things. He actually had a book of photos for me to look through to get an idea of what pattern I wanted my area to look like. The choices included the *Swirl*, the *Landing Strip*, the *Hitler*, the *I Love Lucy* ... you name it, it was all there, in living color no less. I decided to do the real deal, go all the way as they say, as long as I was there.

OK, this first time experience registered a little high on the socially uncomfortable chart, but thankfully Travis was clearly very gay, a professional, and the white Hervé Léger bikini was already out and waiting to be packed for the vacation on the Cote d'Azur. Before beginning, Travis offered me a glass of champagne but I naïvely refused. That makes it sound like a date gone wrong somehow. How bad could it be? I wanted all my wits about me, but it would have surely helped numb the pain. There is that hindsight thing again.

So there I was splayed out on the table like a chicken on a cutting board. Then came the paddle with boiling hot wax dripping from it. He painted on the boiling hot dripping wax, then applied the strip of tape over it and applied gentle pressure so the wax would boil my skin I think. Next came the RIIIIIIIIIIIP of the tape that seemed to take an eternity. There goes the strip of hair, but it's the stinging pain that follows that is the most unforgettable part of the experience. I take that back. It might be when he politely asked me to turn over. Why? I asked myself, but I flipped over. Oh, the ol' "wax up the crack" trick. Nice. I left there feeling like a Chinese Crested, the ugliest hairless dog in the world.

I could not cross my legs or do much else for the next twelve hours, but I expected that, sort of ... but have I mentioned the underarm pain? Seriously, I could not put my arms down. I sat on the sofa with my arms outstretched for two days. So, schedule your appointment for late in the day when you plan to stay at home that evening. Waxing works well for the upper lip and bikini area, however.

Shaving

I like shaving my legs. I must, since I've done it three billion times or more. I do not shave every day, however. Because my skin is sensitive, it works better for me to shave every other day in the winter, and when I can get away with it in the summer. If you are going to the beach, or will have bare legs showing, then by all means shave before going anywhere. There is a lot of area to cover on your legs (including upper legs) so this shaving method is the most efficient: Shave in the shower before you wash your hair. Don't wait too long, otherwise your skin will swell and you won't get a close shave. Choose a shaving cream to suit your skin type. The razor you select should have a multiple blade so you only need to cover the area once. This will reduce the chance of getting razor burn.

Toss your razor blade as soon as it starts to dull to prevent irritation. Rinse the razor well after you use it and store in a dry place to avoid bacterial growth. Shaving works best for your legs and underarms.

The choice of which type of hair removal comes down to what your needs are, and what you can afford. If body hair is really a problem or embarrassment for you then prioritize it above new shoes and anything else until you get it taken care of. If you have excessive hair on your arms or anywhere else, get rid of it. I don't care what nationality you are, it is unbecoming and un-girly in our society, and it can easily be remedied.

Nails

Always keep your nails clean (duh!), and manicured. This is another thing that people notice right off the bat. Avoid gimmicks like paste-ons or glitter unless you are under the age of 12. My favorite polish is a French manicure (most difficult to maintain, but works with any color outfit) or a natural pink like Opi's Bubble Bath, especially in the summer. It just looks clean, fresh and well-kept. Darker colors work well on your toes in the winter when they aren't as exposed as they are in the summer. Generally you need a pedicure more often in the summer than the winter, when your toes are peeking out all the time. Choose a deep red or go as dark as the famous "Rouge Noir" by Chanel. I especially love a dark color on short nails. If you go to darker colors, the polish chips faster, and then looks so tacky. It might be easier and certainly less maintenance to save the bold colors for your toes, or for manicures for a special occasion unless you can indulge in a regular weekly manicure. Shorter nails are easier maintenance and look cleaner and more efficient. Extremely long nails or nails with decoration look high maintenance and trampy. Fingernails and toenails should match, unless you opt for a neutral on your hands.

My manicure trick is to put a thin topcoat on every night before bed, and your manicure can last a week or more, depending on how much gardening, cooking, and other work with your hands that you do. Another trick is to use a white pencil under clean nails to brighten them. I also am addicted to cuticle oil, and apply it before bedtime and more frequently during the winter when my skin becomes dryer. Acrylic nails gross me out. They are expensive, high-maintenance, and toxic. Only do this if you need a temporary fix for a low tear, although there are several other alternatives such as silk for short-term fixes.

Teeth

If your teeth are not straight, and you missed out on getting braces, you should consider them now. Your smile says a lot about you. Nobody likes braces, but all good things take effort, so bite the bullet and just do it. If you lose a tooth or need other dental work, prioritize it. Not only for the way you look, but for your health also. Speaking of health, flossing your teeth after every meal is also an important part of your routine. Now experts are saying it will help the longevity of your life by keeping really creepy bacteria from entering your body. OK, yuk, that sold me on flossing.

Your teeth should not be whiter than the whites of your eyes. Use whitening toothpaste on a regular basis and schedule regular cleaning and checkups. There are so many new products and treatments on the market now there is no excuse for less than bright white teeth. Sell your car or your Manolos if you need to, but your smile oftentimes is the most memorable thing about you. Preventative care is imperative. Brushing and flossing your teeth is a basic as brushing your hair.

After you eat, check your teeth for any food remnants when using the ladies room – not at the table please. Carry floss in your handbag. While we are at it, also, never apply lipstick or anything else at the table. So déclassé.

Skin

Your face is a canvas. Even before you learn to paint it well with makeup, you need to learn to care for its condition. Otherwise whatever you paint over it will be futile. Cleanliness is the most important thing to do to your face. Wash with a mild cleanser morning and evening. Apply toner, unless your skin is very dry or sensitive, then just moisturize. Include your neck in each step, and consider it a part of your face for your entire life. If you've noticed, women with face lifts and lots of cosmetic surgery aren't able to correct the neck, so it is often the telltale sign of a woman's age, as are the back of her hands.

The basic steps to your beauty regimen for the face are:

- Cleanse
- Tone
- Moisturize

You will probably have more products that you add as time goes on, depending on your type of skin and your lifestyle.

If you have particularly dry or oily skin you will need to make adjustments to the routine to suit your needs. I always add in sunscreen before moisturizing. I also add in eye cream at night. My daytime moisturizer is a lighter product then my evening moisturizer. I am over simplifying this entirely, but it is so individual you really need to see an expert at the cosmetics counter to get started, or perhaps to change what you have been using if you are unsatisfied with the results. It takes some fine tuning. The important thing is to BEGIN. Get started, it is never too late and this is critical to feeling and looking good. Do this morning and evening and always take your makeup off before you go to sleep every single day of your life, even when you are at a sleepover.

The skin on your entire body needs care too. Exfoliate. Use a body scrub and a loofah regularly in the shower to keep your skin smooth. Moisturize daily and hit every inch of your skin. The neck and back of the hands are often forgotten, and these areas show aging early. Keep your skin free of skin tags that can appear with aging, and have your moles, freckles and sun spots looked at during your regular checkup. Sometimes these can be removed at the doctor's office relatively easily.

If you are prone to dry skin, I recommend applying bag balm to your feet, elbows, even hands. It is also a great treatment for stretch marks. Use it nightly and wear cotton socks and gloves as often as necessary for an inexpensive and effective way to moisturize (works on hands too, but is a bit thick). By all means, have a regular pedicure. A pedicure is not just about trimming, shaping and polishing your toenails. It is important to tend to the cuticles and remove calluses. Everyone is different, but for me once a month in the winter is sufficient, and twice a month in the summer, since open toed shoes take their toll. In the meantime, I use an exfoliating foot scrub in the shower and the bag balm at night (sometimes adding my cotton socks) and my feet have never been happier.

Let's talk more about feet. If you have corns or bunions, have them taken care of by a podiatrist. They just get uglier and more irritating as time goes on. Athletes Foot, warts and fungus, while gross, are very common. Start with over-the-counter remedies, and if you aren't satisfied with the results, have that podiatrist take a look. And by all means, don't wear revealing sandals until you are able to put your best foot forward.

Makeup

A happy medium is required, not too much, not too little, and less for day, more at night. Have your makeup done professionally by a makeup artist at least once a year as they introduce you to trends, give you helpful hints, and help you decipher what you need in a myriad of product lines. They tend to be a little heavier handed than not. You don't have to buy anything but you will want to buy something though.

At the very least, after you have done your morning grooming ritual, curl your lashes and apply lip-gloss before being seen in public. To simplify it, stay with one product line. These products have been developed to work together. Buy from a reputable cosmetic department and get to know your salesperson. Besides the incredible amount of product knowledge they possess, they will often give you free samples (perfect for travel) and an opportunity to try new things.

My favorite inexpensive cosmetic tricks:

- Mascara – Maybelline (For me, it's *Very Black* waterproof)
- Eye makeup remover + lip protector – Vaseline
- Blemish remover – rubbing alcohol (just a dab applied with a Q-tip)
- Exfoliator – Alphahydroxy lotion
- Bath salt – Epsom's salt
- Foot lotion – Bag Balm
- Nail polish remover – Revlon
- Sunscreen products – Neutrogena

Splurge on:

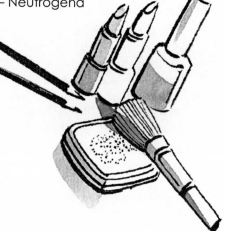

- Cleanser
- Moisturizer
- Concealer
- Eye cream
- Hair products

Then:

- Foundation
- Powder
- Eye Shadow
- Eyebrow Pencil
- Nail Polish
- Makeup brushes
- Blush
- Lipstick
- Fragrance
- Foundation

Foundation can be tricky. Match your skin tone perfectly, don't go darker, no matter how tempting. Depending on the level of your skin's oiliness, dryness, age, and susceptibility to breakouts, you may need concealer, a highlighter, a matte foundation, or one of the numerous other options. I like a light powder application with a big fat powder brush to set the foundation. There should never be a line on your chin or the sides of your face delineating the foundation from your natural skin color.

How much makeup do you feel comfortable wearing? If you prefer a polished look, you'll probably want more coverage. On the flip side, if you don't like the feel of makeup on your face, tinted moisturizers may be your best bet. But beware of versions that are so sheer they don't really do anything to even out the appearance of your skin. It is very important to apply your foundation in natural light or with the help of a lit magnifying makeup mirror. A man must have invented these because you will undoubtedly see things you did not need to know were part of your face. Anyway, start with a small amount the size of a dime and lightly blend along your forehead, nose, chin and cheeks. Blending the foundation outward around the edges of your face and chin will help you to have a natural look and avoid the two-tone skin color of a whiter neck. Foundation is just that, the base layer that helps your skin to look flawless, and holds the rest of the makeup on better.

When choosing your foundation, consider your skin type first. You can reduce shine by choosing a foundation without oil and finishing off with a light layer of powder. If your skin type is dry and sensitive, there are foundations that are richer in emollients to help create a smoother appearance. Foundations now come in so many formulas to offset any skin imperfection. Look for a foundation with a sunscreen too, so you always have some protection. Even when the sun isn't shining, we are still exposed to harmful rays.

Powder

Powder sets the makeup. It should match the foundation and be applied with a big fat powder brush. A really light hand is imperative when applying powder. For older women, or people with oily skin, powder can get caught in the wrinkles and exacerbate the problem, so adjust the application as you age and your skin changes. Just a one, two, three over cheeks, nose and forehead and be done with it. By using powder, your makeup will stay in place longer. You may not want to use powder if your skin is particularly dry, but powder is essential for oily skin types.

Eye Makeup

Your eyes can say it all. I love a dark rimmed eye, but as I've matured I've had to lighten it up for a softer look. Eyeliner frames the eye and brings attention to them. Establish a lighter look for day, and go heavier and more dramatic for evening. Eye shadow defines the shape of the eye. You want to relate the shadow colors to the whole face palette, taking into consideration of course, your coloring, the blush and lip colors, and in fact, your complete outfit.

1. Your eyelid should be clean and dry like a fresh canvas. Apply a medium light color from the corner of your eye outward along the lash line, filling in the lid that closes over the eye.

2. Apply the darkest color on the crease of the eyelid in a back-and-forth motion.

3. Then apply the lightest highlighting color under the eyebrow slightly, blending the edge of the darkest color.

Use a shadow brush or your clean finger for best results. As easy as this really is, it can just as easily all go wrong. I recommend a makeover done by a professional to get started. Be sure to watch in the mirror and have them teach you so you can do it yourself the correct way once you get home. Ask them to write down the product steps.

Your eye makeup shouldn't bleed during the day, so experiment until you get it right. Go back to the makeup artist and sample some different products until you learn what works for you. Take your makeup off religiously every evening before you go to bed.

Eyelashes

Use an eyelash curler, daily. It is another of those inexpensive, quick, natural enhancers that just jump starts your beauty for the day. Shu Umera makes the best eyelash curler on the market, bar none. Use it ONLY when your lashes are clean and free from mascara. If you use a curler with mascara still on it, it can stick to your lashes and potentially rip them out. Wipe the eyelash curler clean after you use it every time. If you do rip out your eyelashes, you will only do it once in your life. This is a fairly common mistake, but it will take you months to recover from this, so heed my warning. First curl your lashes, and then apply the mascara. I recently had a panic call from my friend who had this very thing happen. She was in pain; her eyes were swollen, and even worse, her eyelashes gone. The good news is, the lashes will grow back over several months. If you have short or brittle lashes, try a professional application of extensions. If your lashes are very pale you might have them dyed for a more natural look. Be sure to bat them when flirting, I think this is what they were really made for. I stay clear of lash lengthening mascara because I get fibers in my eyes and is really bothersome.

Eyebrows

Have your eyebrows shaped by a professional and either maintain them yourself intermittently, or schedule regular appointments. Tweezing is the best source of hair removal, for brows, unless they are seriously out of control, then

I would recommend having them waxed. Use a brow pencil that is a shade or two darker than your hair color. Work the brow pencil lightly back and forth softly adding subtle color and definition. It shouldn't look like the lines you drew for eyebrows in Kindergarten. If your brows are too light, have them dyed regularly. They should frame your face, so don't neglect them. A unibrow is a no; gently naturally arched brows are a yes. Painted on eyebrows are a no, gently colored a yes.

Lips

Lip liner is a great product, meant to define and keep your lipstick from bleeding. Lip liner helps you shape your lips however you want, fuller, narrower, more of a bow, whatever. The trick is not to go more than two shades darker than your lipstick – otherwise it looks like trim paint! If you prefer a more natural look, use lip gloss at the very least, but not if you live near the water as gnats will stick to it. I'm fussy about the consistency of the lipstick, not too matte, not too greasy, as well as the fragrance. Mac is my lipstick of choice, but experiment until you find what is right for you. Choose the correct lipstick shade for your skin type. Think of what the rest of the palette looks like on your face and in your outfit and compliment that. Darker colors are more difficult to wear, smear more easily and often need to be reapplied more often. You need a wardrobe of lip colors. A nude beige or pink toned basic is a must. For darker skin, a beige brown color is a good everyday neutral. Expand your repertoire from there. It's fun to experiment, so visit the makeup counter and try colors on. As you get older lighten your lip color. Harsh intense colors like ruby red and vamp age you. They work well against pretty young fresh skin, but do not work against wrinkles and sallow skin.

I like the lip-plumper products – a better alternative to Botox. It's much less expensive and certainly less risky. Look what happened to Catherine Deneuve. That is frightening. The most beautiful woman in the world, and she still didn't think she was beautiful enough apparently. I saw her at a party in Paris to celebrate the opening of a Jean Paul Gaultier store, just before her unfortunate decision of having Botox injected into her lips. Let me tell you, she was absolutely stunning without the puffy lips. That was a bad idea.

Fragrance

Don't overpower, your fragrance should be smelled by the person you want closest to you. Many people are allergic to fragrances and heavily floral fragrances can attract bugs. I don't know if this is scientifically proven, but it is my experience. While we are on the subject, I hate bugs. Granted, they serve their purpose in nature and are oftentimes quite exquisite, but that would be called "off on a tangent." Find a fragrance that you love, and make it your signature. Men will never forget your scent. Choose a winter fragrance that is heavier and more complex and a lighter, crisper fragrance for the summer. It's nice to develop a signature fragrance for each season that is uniquely you. Notice how you and a friend may be wearing the same fragrance but it smells completely different on each other. The beauty department is always happy to give out free samples. Sniff the testers and try some on.

Tanning

... is so gauche. Just get over it. If you read, you know tanning is becoming obsolete. Skin cancer? Premature aging? Tanning not only looks tacky (think George Hamilton), it makes you appear to be completely out of touch. Seriously, be careful – more people are getting skin cancer than ever before. Skin cancer is potentially deadly.

Since I don't lie in the sun in a bathing suit – ever – I have to be careful not to get a "tennis tan," otherwise known as "farmer's tan." That is when you have tan arms and legs half way down. It is difficult to engage in outdoor activities and keep completely sun free. You should have sunscreen in your foundation, and always also apply sunscreen – at least a 30 SPF that blocks UVA/UVB rays – and re-apply every two hours, minimum. Wear a large-brimmed hat, sit under an umbrella or in the shade, and keep your sunglasses on. Keep your face, head, shoulders and chest covered first. Consider investing in SPF clothing. It is work but will be worth the payoff when you are older.

Now we know tanning beds have been found to increase your cancer risk too, so avoid these also. Lying in a tanning bed is like rehearsing in a coffin. Let's face it, the sun feels really good, but we need to retrain ourselves and change the tanning paradigm. A tan does not look healthy. If you still think tanning is pretty, you are terribly misinformed. Stop it! If you just can't get there on your own, there is a crutch. Admittedly, I use them myself in the summer on my legs and arms, but never on my face. I'm talking about bronzing products, or self tanners. They aren't as difficult to use as you may think, the trick is in the application.

- Shower and exfoliate your skin first.
- Do not moisturize where you will be applying the product.
- Spray on self-tanners or bronzers are easier to apply than creams.
- For more intense color, wait ten minutes to apply the second coat.
- But again, we need to work on the paradigm of the Surfer Girl tan.
- Don't go more than two shades darker than your natural skin tone.

I know several people who spray tan. So I tried it. Note to self, do not do this if you suffer from any anxiety disorders. What is with the voice over that filtrates through the sound system? I thought I was about to be beamed up by Scotty.

Scary. I panicked. I ran out of the cylinder, so to speak. Felt dumb, ran back in, followed the instructions that kept barking at me ... right arm outstretched ... weird, futuristic, and inhumane. But there, I did it. A nice, even tan, except for my face, where I squinted my eyes and scrunched up my face in pure angst. I wore a bikini, but wished I had the guts to go nude. I just couldn't help but feel like someone was watching, that voice and all. Anyway, there you go. Spray tans work, and are an option if you are relatively normal and don't suffer from huge neurosis like me.

Posture

Stand up straight. Shoulders pulled back and down and relaxed. Head up as if someone is pulling you up from a string on top of your head. Pull your belly button into your back. Feet slightly apart, pointed straight ahead with your derriere tucked in. Learn Pilates, yoga, ballet or some other physical discipline to get in touch with your body. It will make you feel fabulous besides improving your health and posture.

Take note, the Brittney Spears debacle while exiting a car with her legs wide open was inexcusable, I'm not convinced it wasn't deliberately meant for the paparazzi, but nonetheless, listen up. Her legs should have been glued together as she swung them around to the side then stepped out one foot at a time gracefully. And what ladies don't wear panties?

Then I may as well say it here – always sit with your legs together, too. If you are getting off a stool or chair, glue those gams shut and swing them around. I am truly amazed at the women who don't know this. Mothers with manners, where are you?

So I should also mention, when bending over, bend from the knees, with legs together also. DO NOT, I repeat, DO NOT for any reason bend over from the hips. You might get away with it if you are in pants, but even then it is not a ladylike option.

Fitness

Being fit and feeling healthy are synonymous. You do need to find sports or activities that best suit you. Sometimes it takes trying a lot of different things. I am not a rugged outdoor sports enthusiast, big surprise. I prefer yoga, Pilates, tennis, swimming, walking, and working out with a trainer that I can complain to, and skiing in perfect conditions is what I am all about. The point is, you really do have to sweat to keep the weight off and get the cardio benefits. IPod and video workouts are great if you prefer to work out at home. Alternatively, group and co-ed sports are a wonderful way to meet people while getting a workout. You just have to do it. There are so many ways to get exercise now inside or outside of the gym. Have you ever seen runners smiling? Find the fun. Exercise has a myriad of health benefits as we all know. Establish the routine of exercise as part of your daily regimen and make time for it throughout your life. Don't forget stretching, it feels so good.

Diet

Maintaining good nutrition is imperative to looking good and feeling good, and having those workouts payoff. A healthy diet affects your skin, nails, hair, and ensures good health and can increase longevity. You should know what your caloric intake should be for the type of exercise routine and lifestyle you have and your weight. Then read labels for the caloric count as well as the nutritional values in the food before you buy it, if you don't recognize or understand an ingredient, then pass on it. Pretty soon it will become automatic, and you won't have to obsess if you went off the wagon. I allow myself a piece of chocolate at 4:00 or a scoop of ice cream every day if I want it. I just don't eat chips, sodas, or anything else with sugar, and not much bread. Your plate should have lots of green, red, yellow and orange. Color. If it's all white, you probably are satisfying your hunger with carbs, and you'll be hungry again soon. You'll eat more and more fattening foods.

We've all heard about super-sizing, so be conscious of proportions. One good way to eat less is to eat small size healthy meals or snacks throughout the day. Use a salad plate for dinner instead of a dinner plate. Refuse to have seconds, and drink a few glasses of water or munch on fresh celery or apple slices before dinner if you're hungry. The other thing to be careful of is that daily "grande white chocolate mocha with whip." Find your signature Starbuck's drink that isn't your entire caloric intake for the day.

It is always better to eat the food in its initial stage, such as fresh organic carrots instead of frozen carrot cupcakes. I don't think that really counts as "eat your carrots." Choosing sustainable foods, organic locally grown foods, as close to the source as possible and being conscientious about what you eat and how much you eat is paramount.

Nasty Stuff

Tattoos

Know that I have nothing against tats (I can't believe I even know that word). I just totally lied. I actually hate tattoos. While they have become mainstream and I see them everywhere on everyone, I still associate them with cheap, tacky, low class, and prison gang members. If you can't resist the urge, may I suggest you do something small and selective, and choose a non-public place to display it. No one wants to see it when you bend over in one direction or the other. A much younger and hipper friend told me they were called hooker horns. There you go! Tattoos are a permanent accessory. If you change your mind, they can be difficult and painful to remove. That being said, whatever you do, don't have someone's name tattooed on your body, I know you think he is the one, but trust me, you will likely have several "the one's" in your lifetime.

Body Piercing

My father told me I looked like a gypsy when at 13, I came home with pierced ears. I'd gone downtown to the jewelry store in our small town, the only place then where you could have it done. In retrospect, while I don't regret it and have worn pierced earrings almost every day of my life thus far, I do think piercing is really strange. I find myself fascinated with the cashier who has a pierced tongue – I can't even imagine pierced nipples or labia. Forget about the disk-piercing thing – what is that? It is maiming a perfectly beautiful body part. Potentially disfiguring – gawd, stop it! I've been told by an unreliable source that your skin returns to normal when you stop wearing the disk, but that doesn't make any logical sense to me. Could someone please explain this to me? Never mind, I don't even want to think about it.

Foot Jewelry

Toe rings and ankle bracelets are Icky tacky and cheap. What might possibly be cute at 12 is not-so-cute at 30.

Bare Feet

This is so gross. Imagine all the germs where you are putting your feet. Just because you can't see them doesn't mean they don't exist. You could also step in something icky. Going barefoot will also make your feet really dirty. Barefoot only belongs at the beach, a nice clean beautiful beach preferably an island like Nantucket, in Hawaii, the Caribbean or an even more exotic locale. Best to wear a bare flat sandal or Havianas flip-flops.

Cursing

There is absolutely no excuse for a potty mouth. This speaks to who we are and how we think of ourselves and if it is a habit of yours, lose it. It is not pretty, feminine or educated to talk like a truck driver. And I include trendy words such as "like" here as well. Listen to yourself speak, you may be appalled. You start out thinking you are cool, soon it becomes a habit, then the whole world cringes when you say these words, or at least they should. Words that demean women are inexcusable and intolerable. Our culture is ridden with negative terms for women, so much so that it has become almost mainstream. Do not allow it.

Gum Chewing

My husband grew up in Georgetown, and one day was in the local corner grocer when in walked Katherine Hepburn. In less than a minute, she had walked up to another shopper in the store who was literally chomping, snapping and popping a piece of gum and Ms. Hepburn, without saying a word simply put her hand out under the girl's mouth.

The girl mechanically spit the gum out in Ms. Hepburn's hand, to which Ms. Hepburn declared, "When you chew gum, you look like a horse." Need I say more?

Smoking

Hate it, hate it, hate it. This is such a nasty habit that becomes a devastating addiction. It plain stinks. It makes your hair smell, your body stink, your breath reek, your environs toxic and your friends become victims of your second hand smoke. Oh, let me go on. I have actually seen women spitting from smoking. Yes, s p i t t i n g! It causes wrinkles around your mouth, and is a very expensive addiction to maintain. It affects nearly every organ in the body. Smoking is indeed an addiction, making it extremely difficult to stop without support, and in fact people who start smoking under the age of 21 have the hardest time quitting. Smokers are also more likely to use drugs and alcohol and more likely to have anxiety and depression. If these reasons are not enough to get you to stop, don't forget that it causes fires, lung disease, heart disease, erectile dysfunction in males, and will kill you! It is not cool. It makes you look like an idiot with a death wish who stinks. Get help through a reputable program. It is after all, an addiction, so don't expect to quit on your own. Until then smoking will dominate your life.

Drinking

Watch what you drink and know your limits. A good rule is 0-1-3. Zero if you are driving or are underage, one drink per hour (with food) and no more than three drinks the entire evening. Excessive drinking, like doing anything else to excess, signals that you may have another problem that you are trying to hide or escape from. Figure it out; get help from a therapist and deal with it – it won't go away on its own. Drunk girls are not funny, pretty, or safe. They are pathetic, actually.

Eat before going out, so you have something in your stomach to absorb the alcohol. Figure out which drink your system can handle. Everyone is different, so learn your boundaries and adhere to it. Don't mix types of liquor. Stick to the same drink, and the likelihood of getting sick will diminish. The fun of drinking is that it relaxes you, makes you more outgoing and confident, but it can and does impair your ability to make clear decisions.

Drinking can also make you more emotional and irrational. Never ever drink and drive. Have a buddy plan with a friend you trust. Plan ahead to take a taxi or drive with a friend. Women cannot process alcohol as easily as men (actually just half as much), so don't even attempt to keep up with a guy.

Date rape drugs are real, so a safer solution to accepting a drink might be to pour your own drink, open your own beer, or b.y.o.b. At the very least, know who is mixing your drink and keep it in your hand – don't ever set it down. Never drink alone, and never go off alone with a group of guys you don't know, no matter how cute they are. Do not go into an isolated bedroom at a party, or a car with someone you don't know. Watch out for your friends too, and never leave anyone stranded. And never ever drink tequila. It brings out the evil devil in you.

Drugs

Drugs have additional danger over drinking. Besides being highly addictive, your inhibitions are further lowered; your judgment and the ability to protect yourself are all in jeopardy. If someone has sex with you when you are unable to consent or say no because you are high, drunk or have passed out, you have been raped. If this unfortunately happens to you, and let's hope it never does, you must report it. You will probably help another woman besides helping yourself.

We have all seen families devastated by drug addiction. This doesn't just happen to teenagers. You can become addicted at any age. People aren't making it up and just trying to scare you when they say drugs kill. Drugs can cause or mask emotional problems like anxiety, depression or hallucinations. Either of these illnesses can result in death by suicide or homicide.

Most drugs are highly addictive, so once you start, even after one time, it is very difficult to recover. As difficult as it may seem, stay away from parties or situations where there are drugs. If you feel pressured by a friend to do drugs, they really aren't a friend then, are they? They want company, and justification by you doing what they do. Really, just stop and think. Find new friends who are more supportive to the lifestyle you want for yourself. Surround yourself with positive role models. If you need help, ask for it.

And So On

Most of us do something that annoys other people. Knuckle popping, picking at split ends, biting nails, picking at cuticles or blemishes, slurping, finger tapping, the list goes on and on. You may need help if you can't stop yourself. These habits are unbecoming, unhealthy and annoying to other people. Bad habits detract from you being your best.

Human beings pass gas several times a day. If this becomes embarrassing or obtrusive in any way, pay close attention to your diet. Particular foods tend to cause us to have more gas than others.

While I don't consider putting your hands in your pockets to be quite as bad as the aforementioned habits, this, too, should be avoided. Aside from setting a sloppy, laissez-faire tone, and causing poor posture, it wears on the seams of the garment and can stretch out the pockets. If the pockets come with basting stitches inside them, leave them. You will be less inclined to use the pocket in the first place. Never put heavy keys or other stuff in your pockets, either. Carry a small handbag instead.

You may just have a nervous habit and not be aware that you are even doing it. Recognizing you have a bad habit is one step, and the second step is to find the cause of it. The cause can often give you the answer you need to help rectify it. If you pick at your eyelashes, for example, it may be the lash-lengthening mascara you are using, or you might have an allergy to an ingredient in the mascara. Then you need to do something about it. Ask a friend to take a photo of you when you do it, and hang it on your mirror to remind yourself every day. Be conscious and aware of yourself. There is no need to be self-conscious because you lack self-control.

Here are a few other things I absolutely must mention that are particular pet peeves:

- Private matters should be just that, private.

- Body parts, body functions, body fluids, intimate sexual details, are private. No one wants to hear about yours, hate to tell you.

- I can't tell you the number of times I have been at a cocktail party when some woman forgets she is in mixed company and speaks in elaborate detail about childbirth. Who wants to hear about that? Well, only pregnant women. Please, let's retain some mystery.

- Promise me if someone (typically only men) asks you how many men (or women) you have slept with, respond with a smile, and say "none of your business".

In a civilized society, we do not force the unsightly and badly behaved on others.

Period

First things first: It's so frightening to do the math. I, like most women my age, have spent approximately 2400 days bleeding. That's right, over 6½ years of my life.

First, there's PMS if you, like most women, are so fortunate to experience one of the many symptoms such as mood swings, irritability, anxiety, cravings, fatigue, headaches – oh boy. Pay attention to yourself, and you can begin to identify your symptoms and minimize the risk. Keep a journal or calendar to record how you are feeling when, and what worked to alleviate the symptoms. Chances are there is a pattern to the madness, and you can affect it. There is no reason you need to live your life as a wacko woman when you can be wonder woman.

If you are feeling like your period is getting the best of you, then learn to manage it, too. Proper diet now, especially, affects how you feel. Avoid red meat, refined sugars, caffeine, and alcohol. Eat a diet of high fiber, lots of fruits and vegetables – particularly now. Also very helpful are exercise, stretching, relaxation techniques such as massage, meditation, an aromatherapy bath, a heat pack on your abdomen to ease cramping, over-the-counter medications and even an orgasm can work wonders.

One thing I have learned about being a woman, things continually change. For a while you may have severe cramps and PMS and years later you won't have any symptoms at all. Aunt Flow may be very heavy at times and barely there other times. Our hormones are as much a part of us as water, so learn to recognize the way your hormones make you feel and act. If you are experiencing extremely heavy flow, large blood clots, extreme pain, are feeling out of whack or just odd in general, talk to your gynecologist.

An important thing to know – if you don't already – is to wear a tampon no more than six hours, max, and don't wear a super-absorbent one unless you really need it. Use the lowest absorbency tampon for your particular flow. Wear a pad to bed, not a tampon. Toxic Shock Syndrome, while rare, is life-threatening, so don't abuse these rules. Believe it or not, almost every woman I know has "lost" a tampon at some point in her life. Was it left in and did it disintegrate? Did I take it out and forget? If you start to get a tummy ache, you probably left it in. If you can't find it to pull it out, don't panic, but you should get to your doctor right away.

A few myths about menstruation that you may not be aware of: You CAN get pregnant during your period, and you don't necessarily ovulate every month.

Every woman is unique, certainly. It is your body, so don't let it down. Take the time to figure yourself out, become attuned to what your body is telling you. Listen to your body talk.

B.C.

Birth control should be seriously considered before you begin having sex. Take the time to research your options before deciding on which is best for you. Options include the rhythm method; and barrier methods such as a diaphragm, cervical cap, female condom, and contraceptive sponge, Hormonal methods include "the pill," "the mini pill," the "patch," and the vaginal ring. There are also IUDs and several other options. There is emergency birth control, too, just in case you need it.

Each method of birth control has its pros and cons. The pill, for example, may help reduce menstrual pain and cramping, acne, and excessive body hair. It may also reduce your risk of uterine and ovarian cancer. However, if you smoke, the pill dramatically increases your risk of heart attack and stroke.

All of these options are highly personal with varying degrees of success. It would behoove you to do your research, discuss the options with your gynecologist, and make the choices that are right for you.

I was being fitted for a diaphragm and, when my ob/gyn left me to practice, all hell broke loose. Who knew it created a huge suction, so when I tried to pull it out, I had to get my fingernail under the rim and really tug. It flew like a slippery Frisbee all the way across the exam room, hit the wall and slid slowly down and plopped on the floor. After a pregnant pause, I asked myself, "Did this really just happen"? Obviously, the diaphragm wasn't the appropriate method for me.

No matter what "he" says, withdrawal is ineffective. Even if a man pulls out before he ejaculates, there is still a small amount of fluid that is emitted first. This fluid includes a small amount of semen. It just takes one sperm to mate with your egg to equal a lifetime obligation. So, somewhere between abstinence and abortion there is an alternative birth control that is right for you.

I want to say that while abortion is not an option for many women, it is a last resort for some. Of the women I know who have had them, many are still saddened by it. None, however, are haunted by nightmares and psychosis, as you may be lead to believe. Talk to your ob/gyn for accurate, helpful, confidential information. Alternatively, Planned Parenthood is a terrific, free organization located nearly everywhere that can help you with exams, birth control, STD testing, and abortions. They offer a plethora of information on their website, so it may be a good place for you to start.

Prince Charming

As young girls, we were led to believe Prince Charming would one day arrive on his dashing stead and sweep us off our feet. We would live in a castle, wear gorgeous gowns, and our prince would bring us wildflowers he'd picked on the way home after slaying the enemy. We'd enjoy each other's company and the sumptuous dinner the servants prepared. As we matured, we embellished the story somewhat. We dreamed of our Prince leading us to a sumptuous bed where we made mad passionate love and afterwards declared our undying love and adoration for one another. And the best part, we lived happily ever after.

Wow, was that ever a fantasy. Reality isn't quite like that for me or for anyone I know. It is imperative that when you are young you play the field, date a lot of different kinds of people, and figure out what really attracts you and what qualities in a person matter to you. Be present and aware and never settle for someone who treats you badly. If you get too serious with one person for any length of time, you limit your opportunities to meet other interesting people. Then you become more entrenched in one another's lives and it becomes more difficult to extract yourself. When you spend all of your time with that one boyfriend, you tend to exclude yourself from your girlfriends, too, and that isn't good. Girlfriends give us perspective, camaraderie and friendship. I just hate it when a friend is one of your best friends until she has a steady boyfriend, then she disappears. She resurfaces only when they are breaking up and you are the shoulder she cries on. Not fair.

Back to him and sex. Everyone does it eventually, hopefully. Sex that is. Sex is a beautiful thing when you are in a good place mentally and like the one you are having sex with.

It turns ugly when you aren't feeling good about yourself, the one you are with, or the situation you are in. It is imperative to understand the basics of mating. True, we like to think they are or can be our best friends. Reality check, they can't. I don't have sex with my best friend. Who would I weigh in with?! Men think differently, act differently, and just are, well, different. Men are from Mars, it's really true. They are much more "in the moment" while women think ahead and actually plan. I know, this is a hugely gross over-generalization, but I am sticking to my beliefs. So if you go on a date, have a great time, and don't hear from him ever again, do you understand why? You aren't immediately in front of him. He can't see you. It isn't that he necessarily didn't have a great time too, he is just thinking of the girl sitting in the row in front of him right now. If you were that girl right this minute, you would both be having that great time again. But you aren't there. He isn't thinking of you babe, hard as it is to imagine. It's not that he isn't a nice guy, or that he doesn't like you even. It is just that he is male. That is the difference, in a nutshell. Nice segue. Men plant as many seeds as they can in order to propagate the species. Women have one precious egg a month, and we must be protective of that egg and consequently who we sleep with. Consciously or not, that is real.

So, don't do anything you are uncomfortable doing – either physically or emotionally. If you are alone with a guy, you need to feel 100% OK. Don't let it go too far unless you are willing to go all the way. You can't easily stop a running train. I just heard my mother's voice saying that, but it's so true. Guys are so ruled by their hormones, I mean their penises, actually, and if he remotely thinks he has a chance to have sex with you, he won't give up easily. Have your boundaries established up front, and stick to them. Better that than being swayed by a good-looking guy with a savvy pick-up line and a few Cosmopolitans. He may make you feel bad for saying no, calling you a tease or worse, but stay the course. Don't be "guilted" into going all the way. Trust me, he'll get over it, and no, he won't get "blue balls" or die. His erection can deflate with no harm done to his heart, or yours.

First, before you become sexually involved with someone, you should educate yourself about yourself. Use a hand mirror, (actually) spread your legs and examine your own vulva. Touch yourself, put your finger inside your vagina, and get comfortable with your own body. If you haven't masturbated by now, you should. It is OK. Everyone masturbates. This is just one of those things people are embarrassed about because of bizarre religious beliefs and repressed social mores. It is private and you don't need to tell anyone else. I call it loving yourself. And if you can't love yourself, who can you love? Masturbation will not turn you into a lesbian, or a nymphomaniac. It will teach you how to pleasure yourself, which comes in handy in life. It teaches you about your body and what feels good to you and doesn't. Then you can, in turn, guide your lover towards pleasing you better.

So don't do anything you are uncomfortable with. Sometimes things take some practice, but a good lover should want to please you, too, so gently tell him what you prefer. If a man (or anyone, for that matter,) makes you feel less of yourself, insults you beyond gentle teasing, berates you, or in any way makes you feel less of yourself, you are being verbally abused. I was just told a story of a woman who is married to a wealthy man in Malibu that verbally abuses her. She feels trapped with two children and no career or visible means of supporting herself. OK. Stop right now. First of all, verbal abuse is abuse. It often leads to physical abuse, but verbal abuse is still, unequivocally abuse. He is tearing down her self-esteem, and that is a horrible thing. The money and lifestyle just represent a false sense of security, and does not bring happiness.

Physical abuse includes shoving, pushing, holding you down, hitting, biting, striking you with an object, slamming a door in your face, choking or kicking you, incapacitating you in any way. Don't kid yourself. This is not your fault, you are not the cause of his anger. Leave, get out of there as quickly as possible. From then on, walk the goddess walk. Hold your head high, and know that while you may take a few steps backwards, you may have to make some lifestyle changes in order to have peace, true security and yourself back. You will be much further ahead in the end, however.

Also, understand that this will only get worse, not better. No matter how remorseful he is, how much he cries, pleads, or begs your forgiveness, over time the abuse will begin again. You're already in the cycle of abuse. Tell someone – a trusted friend or family member what is going on. If you are married, stash some money away, consult one of the many fabulous advocacy groups for women, and develop a plan. Do not tell him of your plans. Move out, move away, get to a safe place. This is not your fault, you are the victim now, but you don't have to be the victim forever. You do have a choice. Find your strength and get help immediately. Right on Rihanna did. A lot of women depend on men to support them, but, it is important to be able to support yourself financially. Get a good education, develop a skill, do something that you love. Then it isn't work. Life is full of twists and turns, and we all need to be able to take care of ourselves.

Work gives you the confidence to be self sufficient, so that you won't need a man for his money. Rather, you'll want him for who he is. Big difference. Certainly you will have many relationships, perhaps several marriages, children, parents who become dependent, you name it. Don't be naïve about Prince Charming. He's rare. No matter how much you may want it. Be you own, accomplished, independent, confident woman, and you will be much happier, and therefore able to give back if you are in a relationship. Needy no more! A relationship should give to you, feed you, and lift you up. It's a two way street.

Not everyone needs or wants a Prince Charming either. We may not want it now or ever. That is OK, too. It isn't easy to focus on a career and a relationship at the same time, so it might be better for you to get one going first before you attempt to have the other. For some people a relationship is just too tough, so many women remain single. It doesn't mean you are lesbian if you aren't with a man. Although that is perfectly OK, too, and better to find out sooner than later and hurt someone by living the unauthentic you.

Being Social

Girlfriends are, well, a girl's best friend. Good friends that last a lifetime are hard to come by. When you have a good friend, cherish it and do your best to maintain it, even if you live in different places. Social networking helps staying in touch so much easier, so there is no excuse not to.

Sometimes we will encounter people that we think are friends and then they do something really mean to intentionally hurt us. It is difficult not to take that kind of thing personally, but try not to. It is OK to edit friends and move on. Do your best not to "burn bridges," as you never know when you may need that person to give you a job or give your child a chance to play on the soccer team. It's that ladylike thing again.

No matter what you may have heard before, white lies are OK in certain situations like this. When that mean friend asks you to go somewhere or do something, it is OK to say you have other plans, nicely. Pretty soon she'll get the message. Un-friend her on Facebook, too. Surround yourself with your fans, not your enemies.

I don't buy that a guy can be your best friend, unless he's gay. Then he can be the best friend you will ever have. I think guys really just want to have sex with you, even if neither of you realize it in the beginning. Many of you may beg to differ, but from my personal experience, that is just the way it is, unfortunately.

This brings me to another suggestion, which is, if you are friendly with your girlfriend's boyfriend or husband, stop right now. It is tempting fate and can make your girlfriend jealous. Always cc her, invite her along, include her in on the conversation or she and he could think you have ulterior motives. Save yourself the grief. It is best to avoid being with him alone and never put yourself in a situation that could lead to anyone being able to gossip. Again, think ahead.

Social Networking

When to use two-way communication (personal conversation, telephone, email, texting) verses a social/professional networking site (Facebook, Twitter, My Space, LinkedIn, Plaxo) is important to clarify.

Basically, anything on the worldwide web that nearly anyone can access should be considered a live résumé. Do not post anything that is too personal, such as your year of birth, your address, your phone number, suggestive photos of yourself, how hard you partied the night before. Employers and schools now can check on line to see what you are about, and they do. You will be doing yourself huge, perhaps irreversible damage to your reputation and thus limit your options later on if you post anything derogatory.

This brings me to sexting. Don't do it. You lose total control of the rights to your body. It may seem fun at the moment, and certainly not a big deal, but trust me, Just say NO! It is guaranteed to come back to haunt you.

When you have something to share or discuss of a personal nature, or something that is difficult, talk to that person one on one. The ability to see each other's body language enhances the communication process and you will undoubtedly have a clearer, more effective outcome.

If you have something less emotional but still personal to talk about, use a phone. For brief messages such as trying to meet up or say you are running late, a text works well. If you have factual information to communicate, an email is best. Also, emails are a way to document and save communication.

The business networking sites like LinkedIn and Plaxo allow you to post your résumé and connect and network with a vast amount of professionals. The personal networking sites should also be used as a platform to get your résumé/profile out to as many people as possible. Just take a professional stance, and ask yourself this question before you post anything, "Is this something I would want a future employer to read?" If the answer is yes, then go ahead and post it. If you must write something personal, use the inbox and send it like an email, so others do not read it. Don't post it on your wall. Think of your wall as a party. Listen, start and engage in conversation, but again, not too personal.

Personal networking sites are a good way to connect with old friends, meet new people, and tell your entire network something at the same time. It is efficient from that standpoint. Monitor your frequency on Facebook or your "friends" may hide you because it's annoying. It is easy to get carried away and become obsessive, so establish your boundaries for usage. Perhaps 15 minutes at the same time each day, or 2x per week for ½-hour each, something like that. Be choosy about who you ask to be your "friend," as well as which "friend" requests you accept. Be pleasant, professional and use social networking sites to project your image.

Speaking of your image, there are tricks to putting your best foot forward in photographs. With so many opportunities to have your photograph plastered all over the web, here are a few tips to make sure you've got your best shot:

- Act natural.
- Don't hold your breath, but do put your shoulders back, suck in your stomach.
- Bend your arms and legs or you'll look stiff and unnatural.
- Rest most of your weight on your back foot and turn your hips and shoulders slightly. This will help you look slimmer.
- Vary your facial expressions so you have some with big smiles, grins and pouts in your repertoire so you don't always look the same in every photo, and experiment to find your best poses.
- Keep your chin up, head slightly tilted, and don't squint your eyes when you smile.
- This sounds really weird, and feels even weirder, but trust me – practice in front of the mirror first, then take pictures of yourself or with a friend until it becomes second nature.
- Watch the celebrities being photographed on the red carpet. Notice the ones who get the pose thing down. It is what separates the stunning from the dowdy. You can convey whatever look or emotion you want via your photo, so build up a repertoire once you have your default pose down to a science.

Parties

Going To a Party

Eat a little something before you go, even if it is a dinner party. You'll be able to avoid floating in alcohol if those cocktail trays go by too fast. It is polite to take a hostess gift to someone's house. Some favorites:

- guest soaps
- scented candle
- chocolates
- flowers or flowering plant
- hand lotion
- bath oil
- a nice bottle of wine – don't expect it to be served that evening
- a special bottle of olive oil, balsamic vinegar, or sea salts or tea
- a favorite book

Always keep in mind the hostess's taste. The gift need not be expensive, just thoughtful. Be sure to include a small enclosure card with a thoughtful sentiment. It should be beautifully wrapped, as packaging is the first impression. If you don't know how to tie a beautiful bow, learn. Many stationary stores offer classes on gift-wrapping. Never bring "a dish" unless it is a potluck (which I hate!) or the hostess asks you to. Be sure you have the address, time, and all the details ahead of time so you don't have to call the busy hostess as she receives her guests.

Try to meet as many new people as possible, stopping long enough to get to know a little bit about each guest. Say something memorable, compliment them, and smile. It is OK to excuse yourself to move on to other guests. Just say something like "I hope to see you again." Hopefully, you won't be the first to arrive or the last to leave. If you do arrive early, be one of the first to leave. If you arrive later you can leave a little later. You won't overstay your welcome this way, and you won't look lonely and desperate for company, always find your hosts when you arrive to say hello, and again when you are leaving to thank them for the lovely time.

You know never to go to a party or bar alone without telling someone where you are going and who you are meeting, including a phone number or contact info of some.

Giving A Party

Hosting a party is hard work, but terrifically rewarding and lots of fun. Have a strong theme and a good plan and you will have even more fun.

- What is the occasion?
- What is the theme?
- Who do you want to invite?
- Where will the location be?
- When's the date?
- Define the decor
- Create the invitation
- Select the menu

Being a gracious hostess takes some practice, at least it has for me anyway. The more you can do ahead, like clearing the coat closet, arranging the flowers, ordering the catering or preparing as much of the food ahead of time, the easier it will be the day of the party. I always like to have the candles lit, wine opened, music playing, then sit down for 10 minutes or so before the guests begin arriving. Be sure to personally greet the guests as they come, while someone else helps to take their coats and offer them drinks. Introduce them to someone right away and say something about what they do, or how you met, to give them a point from which to take the conversation. Then move on to the next guest. I never have anything to drink until the food (either hors d'oeuvres or dinner) has been served. I need all my wits about me, and can't relax until then anyway.

I keep the next morning schedule open to clean up. This is the rare exception I make to making sure the dishes are done before I go to bed at night. Don't try to do the dishes while your guests are still there. It puts a damper on the evening and may make your guests feel like they need to help. Remember, they are your guests. If you can, hire someone to help you prep, help during the party to poor drinks and to help clean up. You will have way more fun.

Be prepared for some sort of disaster. I hate to be a naysayer, but at nearly every party, some drama has unfolded. Recently someone got a little too tipsy and spilled red wine all over my carpet (white) and unbelievably, the walls (white), as well as on someone's dress (also, white). Needless to say, red drinks are off the list for my parties now. What can you do though? More importantly, never let anyone drive home drunk. Either ask someone to take them home, or call a taxi. How horrible would it be if something were to happen?

Courtesies

We all know how to greet people. First look them in the eye, say hello, and shake their hand with a moderately firm grip and two shakes. When meeting someone for the first time, be sure to say your first AND last name to each person you meet. We all know to say please when asking for something, and to say thank your when receiving something. People are flattered when you are interested in them, so ask questions. You'll probably discover you have a lot in common with them and end up having an interesting conversation.

Just be nice, it's so simple. Try complimenting someone, and watch his or her face light up. Make their day and it will, in turn, make your day, too. If you are in a bad mood, stay home. Don't spread your misery around.

Here are my bugaboos:

- Don't crowd in line, push or shove.
- Don't cut in front of other cars, wait your turn and use your blinker.
- Don't talk on your cell phone in a public place.
- Leave your phone in your handbag, no catching up on emails or texting either.
- Always tip. If you can't afford to tip your manicurist, you can't afford the manicure.
- If you are a house guest, don't make yourself at home.
- Be punctual for appointments.
- If you don't have anything nice to say, don't say anything at all.
- Don't chew gum in public.
- Expect a gentleman (yours, most importantly) to stand up for you when you enter or exit a room, open and close doors for you, and walk on the street side of the sidewalk.

Keeping It All Straight

I once celebrated a fabulous birthday in New York hosted by my favorite fashion designer friend with several of his celebrity friends as guests. Meeting Ivana Trump was, well, priceless. That conversation "vas fahntasteek." When I asked her how she kept up her 11 homes, she named them all, "Vell, I haf homes in Gstaad, Palm Beach ..." I lost track after seven. "Oh it's really not that hard ... of course each of my homes haf a Major Domo to look after the chef, gardeners ..."

Then she went on about her businesses including: real estate, her line of cosmetics and fragrances, being a spokesperson, public speaking engagements – in other words, the endless empire of Ivana. Not only did she look incredible close up and in person, she was incredible. Anyway, my point is – yes I actually have a point – things don't just happen, and success doesn't just land in our lap. She works extremely hard. Like Ivana, it pays off to be organized, to establish your own network of professionals. This includes your hairdresser, dry cleaner, dog walker, manicurist, whomever it takes to make your life run smoothly and efficiently with people to depend on. We may not all be Ivana, but we can learn to be organized, to delegate, to have that team of people we depend on to help our lives run efficiently, and to work as hard as we possibly can to be our absolute best.

When you have a family, it helps to keep everyone's schedules on a master calendar. I use a different color for every person and for my individual appointments – personal or business, I highlight my items with pink, my middle son's with blue, my husband's with green. If I need to be somewhere with them it is pink. I want to know where they are, but unless it is in pink I don't need to worry about getting there. This may seem like a huge effort, but trust me, the time it takes to update it is nothing compared to being late for an important date or missing a big event in your loved one's life. Also, always look a month, week and a day ahead. That way you are not caught out for the day and your child needs his soccer gear or you need to go straight from work to a dinner and forgot the babysitter. I always look at the next day's agenda the night before so I can plan what I will wear, and get everything else set out and organized. There is nothing worse than rushing around like a banshee in the morning and then forgetting something important. Being a competent mother, wife, businesswoman, and whatever else you may be or are about to become, requires daily attention and preparation. The more time you take to be organized and prepared ahead of time, the easier your life will become, and the more free time you will carve for yourself. Not only that, you will look gorgeous at the same time and WOW! There is nothing better than impressing you.

Hit Send

Walk with confidence, one high-heeled foot in front of the other, and move your hips, not your shoulders. Let your arms swing naturally; hold your back straight and your head high. It's the goddess walk, and girlfriend, that's you. Project your whole package. Enjoy the moment, as well as visualize the life you want, believe it will come to fruition, and do the very best with what you have been given. Do something for someone else, every single day of your life. Be kind, caring and loving and it will boomerang back to you. Work it, work it, work it; and you can indeed have it all!

I hope this book has inspired you to become your best.

Acknowledgements

To my beloved mother, for encouraging me to have high standards and always insisting I dress for church in my Sunday Best Dress, matching hat, handbag and gloves. "Sit still and act like a lady" rings in my ears to this day.

With love and appreciation to my prince, John Jacobsen, for his humor, patience, and wisdom. My heartfelt love to our boys, Henry, Johnny and Mads, who think I'm from another planet and have no idea what I am talking about – ever. I'm confident they will all make loving partners though, with good manners.

Special thanks to Zang Toi for his brilliance, generosity and friendship. To Carmen Marc Valvo for his kind heart and clear talent. To Ed Merklin, my heartfelt appreciation for his keen talent, discerning eye and always-fabulous shoes. Thank you to Cherie LePenske for her enthusiastic optimism, Linda Bray for her cleverness, Pamela Raley for her experience and intuition, and to my sister, Gretchen, for leading the way.

Many thanks to the inspirational girlfriends in my life who "get it" and always make me lol: Sally Armstrong, Linda Bonica, Julie Bridgham, Kathleen Clapp, Andrea Gradwohl, Becky Gray, Kelly Norris, Marsha Sleeth, Carol Steele, Erin Tanaka, Stephanie Veka, Katherine Vincent, Robin Winstead, Laurie Yawn.

Oh, and Kevin Dodge.

Bisous!

LaVergne, TN USA
23 April 2010
180393LV00002B/2/P